BE ONE,
BE BEAUTIFUL!

Be One, Be Beautiful!

A call to unity

Mike J. Parnham

DEDICATION

To the memory of Peter Mackenzie, a Baptist, Pentecostal, and Methodist pastor who humbly and lovingly related to other Christians, not on the basis of their labels, but through the bond of peace. He demonstrated the practical reality of Christian unity and planted seeds for the blessing of the Church in Croatia.

Endorsements

This is a passionate outcry for reconciliation and the overcoming of divisions. Mike Parnham emphasizes that Church unity is God's unique method to reveal His love to the world. He calls for a halt to our parochial thinking so that we gain an enlarged vision for "the glorious whole." Coming from an Evangelical background, Mike rescues a biblical concept of ecumenism by including into his vision Anglicans, Catholics, Pentecostals, and even Orthodox believers without any fear of contact. Unity for Mike is not a question of agreement, but a matter of being family. Unity does not result when we share the same doctrines, but when our faith in the blood of Jesus and the power of the Holy Spirit is realized—in spite of all our differences in our Sunday services, in our everyday lives, and in our relationships. He appeals to all churches and denominations to make humility and forgiveness the unavoidable gate into this common "house" of unity.

Diakon Mag. Johannes Fichtenbauer
Director of the Catholic Diocesan Seminary
for Permanent Deacons in Vienna, Austria
Chairman of the Ecumenical Round Table for Austria

For as long as I have known Mike Parnham (about seven years), he has had a passion for unity in the Body of Christ. He not only talks about it, but actively pursues it in his life and ministry. He is able to see the bigger picture from Heaven's perspective that so many, due to working exclusively within their own denominations, cannot. My hope is that Mike's book, *Be One, Be Beautiful!* will inspire many to change the way they view other movements, to pursue loving their brothers and sisters in other ministry streams as Jesus does, and to truly embrace each other in the spirit of unity. If unity in the Church universal is important to you, you will be inspired to action by Mike's book. Enjoy!

Mike Chandler
International Missions
Bethel Church, Redding, California

Unity, that is, the loving-kindness with which those who belong to Christ reach out to others regardless of differing traditions, is the basis for true Christian witness, maintains Mike Parnham in his book, *Be One, Be Beautiful!* He states emphatically that he is writing as a non-theologian to dedicated Christians of all churches and all walks of life. He has no other agenda than to call Christians to notice that in a world whose "DNA" is egoism and fragmentation, the "DNA" of the Kingdom of God—which is love and unity in diversity—is amazingly attractive. Our speaking and disputing about matters of faith is most likely to go unnoticed by the world. Acting in unity from our own churches and background is what the world will find attractive. I hope this book will ignite many sparks in the darkness of this world so that people can stop "stumbling around the dark cobbled streets" and be led by the Light.

Dr. Ksenija Magda, Lecturer in New Testament,
Theological Faculty "Matthias Flacius Illyricus"
Zagreb, Croatia

How good and pleasant
it is when brothers
live together in unity!

Psalm 133:1

Table of Contents

PREFACE

If someone had told me, fifteen years ago, I would write a book on Christian unity I would have found it hard to believe! Back then, I thought of unity, more as an extension of the local church fellowship than as a basis for all Church life. More recently, God has challenged me to reconsider. I am now convinced that the way Christians behave toward one another, particularly toward those of other denominations or groups, plays a fundamental role in God's plan. I hope and pray that this book will help you understand my change of heart and make an honest appraisal of your own attitude toward Christian unity.

The book is the culmination of lessons I now realize I have been learning for most of my life. Like many other Christians, studying at university exposed me to believers of many different colors, in contrast to the somewhat monochromatic home church environment I had experienced. I am certainly indebted to the many friends who opened my eyes to new spiritual possibilities. During the course of a varied professional scientific career, regular attendance, membership, and leadership of fellowships of various denominations across Europe has further broadened my outlook. Together with my wife, Elaine, I have had opportunities in Croatia to apply many of the lessons learned. In fact, many of the concepts I discuss here are as much hers as mine, and we have worked through many of them together.

It is impossible to thank all those who have influenced our thinking on unity, but some names I have sprinkled throughout the book. I thank God for them and all the others who have accompanied us on the various stages of our geographical and spiritual odyssey. I have dedicated the book to the memory of Peter Mackenzie, who for me embodied the principle of Christian unity in bringing together churches across Yugoslavia and its subsequent heritage countries. I am also grateful for the constructive criticism and insights provided by my lawyer son Philip who read through several draft versions. In the final version, I have also taken into account the many helpful comments provided by my brother Andy, a pastor and doctor. I am also indebted to Pietro Evangelista and his colleague Berhanu Workineh at Destiny Image Europe for their support and efforts to get this book into print, and to Esmé Bieberly for her excellent editing.

Zagreb, 2011

CHAPTER 1

THE GREAT OMISSION:
AN APPEAL FOR UNITY

THE MOST IMPORTANT PREREQUISITE
TO WORLD EVANGELIZATION AND REVIVAL
IS THE UNITY OF THE BODY OF CHRIST.

—Paul E. Billheimer, 20th century U.S.
evangelist, broadcaster, and author

Bill is a cheerful, sociable person, always ready with a harmless joke or to play around with his increasing circle of grand- and great-grandchildren. He has a deep, evident love for the Lord and, now into his nineties, is still sought after for his advice and spiritual insight. As a young man, Bill's family lived next to the Johnsons, a Roman Catholic family. Frank Johnson, like Bill, was a musician, and they enjoyed jamming with their jazz band on a Saturday. On Sundays, they went their separate ways to church—Frank to Mass and Bill to the local Baptist church. But this made no difference to their friendship. The Johnson household was like a second home to Bill, and he learned to respect their kindness and moral way of life. Over the years, Bill traveled around as an engineer and met a variety of different Christians. He was a Sunday school teacher and eventually a deacon in the Baptist church; when his children were already adults, he met God in a new way and joined the charismatic house group movement. But you will not ever hear Bill disparage another believer because of his different approach to his faith—and I have known my father-in-law for nearly forty years.

A pastor we knew from a charismatic fellowship in another country, however, would regularly preach against the Roman Catholic church in his sermons. Other leaders in his church readily attended interdenominational meetings of local church leaders, but the pastor was conspicuous by his absence. His confrontational style masqueraded as "being radical" and led to splits with other Protestant churches, including those in the national charismatic movement. Finally forced to move on, he still rails against the evils of other groups and religions.

Over the centuries, Christians have repeatedly rekindled the old hostilities between denominations and rebuilt new walls. In one town in Southern Germany, a few years ago, a physical brick wall was built down the center of a church building so that it could be used by separate Protestant and Roman Catholic congregations! Hiding behind our theological barricades, we have no time for those who do not see eye to eye with us. Protestants snipe at Catholics, Baptists at Methodists, and the Orthodox Church is targeted by everyone. Rather than glorifying Jesus, the world gets hit in our crossfire. What does it achieve? Is the search for theological purity all that matters? Our lack of interest in unity is, in my opinion, the Church's Great Omission. I was impressed by two books, written in an affirmative style, that have been published on the subject in the last half century.

In one of these books, Paul E. Billheimer wrote, nearly 30 years ago,

> The continuous and widespread fragmentation of the
> Church has been the scandal of the ages. It has been
> satan's master strategy. The sin of disunity probably

has caused more souls to be lost than all other sins combined.[1]

Disunity, according to Billheimer, is not just an unfortunate fact of church history. It is sin! It paints a completely wrong picture of Christianity, reflecting human intolerance instead of the glory and love of God.

Dividing us into isolated groups, the enemy effectively disables and demoralizes the people of God. He may use active aggression and persecution, but a much more subtle and effective weapon has been to turn Christians against each other. Separated into like-minded groups, cherishing our own limited interpretations of doctrine, we become so convinced of our arguments that we no longer listen to alternative points of view. Once each fraction considers itself the last remaining defender of the faith, the enemy has won.

God wants His people working *together* to actively initiate change, and praise God, many churches have recognized this and are demonstrating our unity in a practical way. In the United Kingdom, Australia, Uganda, and Argentina, particularly, young people are showing that traditional denominational boundaries can be broken down. A Ugandan friend told us that a crucial factor in the revival in her country was that churches actively sought to be united.

Reconciliation and unity have always been high on God's agenda. Referring to the separation between Jews and Gentiles, Paul says that "He Himself [Jesus] is our peace…and has destroyed the barrier, the dividing wall of hostility…His purpose was to create in Himself one new man…thus making peace" (Eph. 2:14-15). Jesus died to break down the barriers that divide believers and to enable Christians of all confessions to live in peace with one another. He wants us to be visibly united.

GOD'S DYNAMIC VISUAL AID

I really enjoy photography and, as is often said, a picture is worth a thousand words. A child crying, a sheep struggling to escape a flood, a tree bending in a gale, or a young couple embracing—these can all be very eloquent images. When we as Christians show practically that we care for each other, we provide to the viewer a snapshot of God's love. Throughout this book, I shall consider a number of the visual aids the Bible presents of the Church. To start with, I want to address the two most commonly cited, the Body and the Bride.

Recognizing the Body

In the Protestant tradition, we often hear about personal commitment to Jesus and the "priesthood of all believers" (see 1 Pet. 2:9). The main emphasis is on bringing our private lives into line with God's standards and glorifying the Lord by our personal witness. While it is clearly vital that we each develop an individual walk with God, this has to be accommodated into the concept of a united Body.

Paul did not have the benefit of modern medical science, but he did recognize the interdependence that exists within the human body:

> *Just as each of us has one body with many members, and these members do not all have the same function, so in Christ we, though many, form one body, and each member belongs to all the others* (Romans 12:4-5).

Today we know that each cell of the human body contains the same DNA. If it becomes infected by a virus, this can affect the healthy functioning of the whole body. Each organ, limb, and blood vessel is made up of millions of individual cells, and each diverse part carries out a well-defined and unique role. Following this pattern, our individual contributions are of greatest value when they promote the health of the whole Body of Christ.

Applied to the local church, the body principle is often used to encourage the laity to get involved in church activities, according to their spiritual and natural gifting. In recent years, this delegation has proved to be a catalyst for church growth, but it tends to ignore the wider Church, the other believers in a city. We also have a responsibility toward other sections of the Body of Christ. Bearing *all* the churches in our cities in mind,

> *God has arranged the parts in the body, every one of them,*
> *just as He wanted them to be. If they were all one part,*
> *where would the body be? As it is, there are many parts,*
> *but one body* (1 Corinthians 12:18-20).

If we apply the body analogy citywide, one group may be particularly gifted in praise and worship, another in reaching out to the practical needs of their neighborhood. Whether struggling or highly successful, they are all limbs and organs in the one Body of Christ. Dislocated body parts do not reflect the Body as a whole. Alone, they may see growth and be respected, but church unity, not individualism, is God's unique method to reveal His love to the world. We must stop thinking parochially and see our local groups as part of the glorious whole, a concept that we shall develop as the book progresses.

A Powerful, Loving Church

Unity is powerful because it sets a godly example that goes against the social norm. Jesus prayed that *"all of them* may *be one,* Father, just as You are in Me and I am in You"* (John 17:21). This is amazing! Jesus wants to see us, the entire people of God, miraculously incorporated into the oneness of the Godhead. This is supernatural—a level of unity that can only be achieved with the help of the Holy Spirit with the ultimate goal "that the world may believe that You have sent Me...and have loved them even as You have loved Me" (John 17:21,23). In other words, our unity sets God's love and power free and enables others in our city to believe. A united Church is God's dynamic visual aid, a reflection of who He is, because as First John 4:8 tells us, "God is love."

Self-centeredness, however, is the hallmark of our Western society. Postmodern philosophy claims there is no absolute truth. Whatever works best for each individual is all "the truth" we need to know. According to current attitudes, to modify our own desires for the good of others makes no sense, nor do long-term future goals. We see the consequences of this line of thinking all around us in the breakup of marriages, dysfunctional families, violence in society at large, and rampant loneliness. Even the biblical concepts of truth and love are being redefined to suit these inclinations of modern thought.

God wants His Church to transform these entrenched thought patterns and make a profound impression on the selfish behavior of our day. Since non-believers have no idea what goes on inside church walls, we must take the message out. Jesus set us the example of finding and helping people in need. Practical concern for those in our neighborhoods and a deliberate focus on stable marriages and loving relationships in Christian families will enable others to see the love of God in ways conventional preaching cannot present. Most of all, the miracle of Christian unity, particularly in parts of the world where sectarian violence has been rife, will convince sceptics of the truth of the Gospel when well-formulated arguments cannot. When believing and practicing Christians from diverse backgrounds work together, allowing love, not hatred to flow, then an unbelieving world will "believe that You sent Me [Jesus]...and have loved them even as You have loved Me" (John 17:21,23). To ignore the relevance and power of a united Church is to misinterpret the times in which we live.

The Blushing Bride

I am convinced that God is challenging His people everywhere to demonstrate the "oneness of the Spirit" Jesus prayed for at the end of His life on earth. The Church is not only the Body of Christ on earth. One day Jesus will return, and when He does, He wants to find a "radiant Church, without stain or wrinkle or any other blemish" (Eph. 5:27). He is waiting for a Bride "suitable" for Him, one competent to sit on the throne and reign together with the King of kings (see Rev. 3:21).

Several of Jesus' parables deal with the period of preparation between His ascension into Heaven and His coming again in glory. In them, He compares Himself to the bridegroom eager to celebrate His wedding feast. The preparations are underway. The bride is making herself ready. Some of the invited guests are well-informed about their roles; others are ill-prepared or actually refuse to attend (see Matt. 22:1-14; 25:1-13).

As anyone with married children knows, there are few periods in life that strain family relations more than the run-up to a wedding! Not only are the bride's nerves on edge, her whole family is stretched emotionally and financially. Many decisions have to be made and questions answered, including, "Whose wedding is this—the bride's, the groom's, or the parents' financing the festivities?" The reception can be a nightmare—not only the menu but the seating arrangements have to be well thought through. Certain people cannot possibly sit at the same table. A successful celebration requires great diplomacy and tact. We are also called to work together to make Jesus' wedding feast a success, however difficult the united effort might be.

When He returns for His Bride, Jesus wants her to be fully prepared for the wedding, looking beautiful, "holy and blameless" (Eph. 5:27), reflecting His glory (see 1 John 3:2). Often though, rather than being concerned about our beauty treatment, we are so busy with camps and committees, coffee bars and conferences that we do not notice, let alone deal with, our "spots and wrinkles." The Church's public face has many blemishes. We may try to hide them, but the world around us is not blind. They know we are not "holy and blameless" and avoid us. It is time we unveiled the beauty of the one Bride, so that she fully reflects the glory of the Savior who redeemed her.

REFLECTING OUR FATHER'S GLORY

I am neither a theologian, nor am I involved in full-time Christian work (which I hope will be an encouragement to the majority of readers). I am a research scientist approaching the end of an international career, during which we lived in both Western and Eastern Europe. As a "grassroots Christian," it was not always possible to find a local church that fit my own inclinations and preferences. I think this is probably one of the best things that happened to me! Getting to know other Christians as people, I recognized that despite our different ways of seeing things, those who love and serve Jesus all belong to the same family of God. As a result, my attitude to the Church as a whole has been broadened, and my prejudices toward other believers corrected—not simply by worshiping together on Sundays.

A Diverse Family

In a functioning family, opinions and attitudes between the members can vary considerably. *Believers do not have to agree about everything.* In fact, as we shall consider later, it is my conviction that unity in diversity brings more glory to God than any artificial conformity. We do not all have to go to the same sort of church. It is our attitude toward other members of the family of God that is important. Unity in diversity requires the acceptance of those who see things differently from us and have different expressions of belief. God wants to weave believing Catholics and Anglicans, Pentecostals and Brethren together in His all-consuming plan. As Paul told us, "God has arranged the parts in the body, every one of them just as *He* wanted them to be" (1 Cor. 12:18). Jesus made it clear what God's plan is.

Jesus' Prayer for Our Unity

Shortly before He died, Jesus spoke these words:

> *I pray also for those who will believe in Me…that all of them may be one, Father, just as You are in Me and I am in You…. I have given them the glory that You gave Me, that they may be one as We are one—I in them and You in Me…may they be brought to complete unity. Then the world will know that You sent Me and have loved them even as You have loved Me (John 17:21-23).*

It has to be significant that just before He went to the cross, what was uppermost on Jesus' mind was the unity of His disciples—those who had accepted His teaching and offer of eternal life and believed Him to be the Son of God sent by the Father (see John 17:2,8). These were committed men and women of God. His prayer also included those who would believe throughout history—that is, you and me! (See John 17:20.) Jesus knew in advance that it would take a miracle to mold and hold committed believers together. Fully aware of the magnitude of the task, Jesus had already promised, "I will ask the Father, and He will give you another Counsellor to be with you for ever—the Spirit of Truth" (John 14:16-17).

The level of unity Jesus requires from His followers is not humanly possible—how could it be? It was comparable to the relationship between God the Eternal Father and His Son. Only the Holy Spirit can lead believers into a true understanding of their high calling. This is why Paul writes in First Corinthians 12:13, "We were all baptised by one Spirit into one body…and given the one Spirit to drink." I do not believe he is referring simply to the rite of water baptism, practiced in different forms throughout the Church and often more divisive than unifying. The Holy Spirit is pictured here as incorporating us into the Body (immersing us) and being present within us (as a drink). The underlying thought in this verse is that all true believers have been supernaturally "saturated with one Spirit."[2]

But unity was not only close to the heart of Jesus during His last days on earth. His prayer reveals that it is also linked with His eternal *glory* (see John 17:22). Why? Because unity reflects God's character as nothing else can. God is one, yet intrinsically Father, Son, and Holy Spirit. Jesus consistently emphasized His unity with the Father and the Spirit, despite Their mysterious distinction. As God is love, so each part of the Trinity is a reflection of that same love. Our unity with Jesus and with each other, therefore, miraculously mirrors the love that exists in the Godhead. It is a sign to the world of the Father's all-consuming love and is, as such, living proof that Jesus' teaching is true. None of our local congregations or parishes preaches the whole counsel of God. Like the many different facets of a polished diamond, we each make a contribution to the beauty of the whole but need each other to reflect the entire and glorious truth.

It is my growing conviction and the central message of this book that the purpose of the Church is not, as is widely preached, to defend the doctrinal purity of the Scriptures or to keep ourselves from worldly pollution (though, of course, these should not be ignored). Nor is it primarily to obey the Great Commission to go out into the whole world and preach the Gospel! *The Church is in the world to reflect the glory of God as Jesus Christ did. United in love, she is part of God's message, not simply the messenger.* In other words, unity is not optional; it is vital.

A Vision of Frost

About five years ago, during a time of prayer, the Lord gave me a picture of a window pane covered by a glaze of pure, white frost. Admiring the intricacy of the swirling, fern-like patterns, I knew this masterpiece had not developed from one central point. A mass of disconnected filigree patterns, scattered across the pane, had spread out toward each other to transform a plain glass window into a magnificent work of art. By analogy, God assured me that He was on the move and would be glorified in the city of Zagreb, Croatia, where I was living. He convinced me there were many other like-minded but scattered groups of believers all praying for the nation. It was vital to find and encourage each other. We did not have to abandon our existing groups or try to persuade one another to pray or behave differently. Unity meant being one in Spirit, part of the same team, acknowledging and respecting one another, not competing. Like the prophet Amos, our prayer for Zagreb was to be, "Let justice flow like a river [through Zagreb] and righteousness like a never failing stream" (Amos 5:24). If the Church was willing to be united in prayer, God promised that He would hear and answer.

We soon discovered that it was true: we were not alone. Not only have churches of the Reformation tradition been drawing closer to one another in recent years,[3] some Roman Catholic believers have been praying for as long as twenty-five years for the unity of Christians in our city! God is at work in Croatia. I firmly believe that He is building *His* Church here to be a light to the divided Balkan nations.

Perhaps many of us feel alone as Christians because we have never taken the trouble to find other believers in our neighborhoods or workplaces. Perhaps we think that only those who belong to our particular church and adhere to our tenets of faith are the "chosen ones." We tend to forget that no group, however spiritual or knowledgeable, is the sole purveyor of truth. Often we have never even checked whether there is another Christian where we work. One may be Protestant and the other Catholic, and so we have generally avoided each other. If we both believe in the power of Jesus' blood to save, starting to pray together for those around us can be a mutually encouraging experience. How about meeting for coffee with the neighbor, starting a weekly prayer group at work, or even getting together to redecorate a pensioner's home? God is in the business of growing small seeds.

So That the World May Believe

Fellow believers are brothers and sisters, not the opposition. Our church walls have divided us, but *there is only one Church as far as Jesus is concerned, and it is His, not ours!* It is time to extend the hands of friendship to those who truly belong to Jesus, even when their doctrine differs from ours. We do not have to convert them to our way of thinking but pray together, encourage one another, and work in our neighborhoods, towns, and cities. Jesus prayed that we can and should be one, despite our differences of opinion and doctrine. We must seek to remain united in the Spirit, "so that the world may believe" (John 17:21).

Charles Colson and Ellen Vaughn, in their book *Being the Body*, provide a detailed treatise on the role of the Church.[4] It caused intense debate in the United States and some other countries. Reading the many testimonies they share of how God has been breaking down barriers between Christians further confirmed to me that God is speaking the same message in many different countries. We cannot allow ourselves to be deaf to His call. We will have to let go of our preconceived ideas about religious divisions that are no longer relevant, but often a hindrance. Then we can begin to restore broken relationships between churches and families, since reconciliation to God and to our brothers and sisters in Christ across our cities and nations is the recipe for a strong and healthy Church. It is essential that we get things sorted out with God and our fellow believers—whatever their doctrine and confession—and start tuning into the Holy Spirit.

I believe we need to follow Paul's advice in Romans 12:2 and allow the Holy Spirit to transform us by renewing our minds. We must avoid making generalizations based on doctrinal differences. Just because there is no fellowship of your denomination in a particular town does not make all the citizens unbelievers and in need of salvation! We must open our minds to the fact that God has His faithful servants in a wide variety of churches, denominations, and walks of life. Many of those who hold different doctrines are true believers. They are our brothers and sisters who deserve our love and care. God is Love. Love is relational, not theological. In eternity, the Bride will be worshiping and serving the Lord as one, ruling over kingdoms in the new creation, judging angels. She will not be debating theology!

In First Corinthians 13:4-8, as we shall study later in more detail, Paul describes what love really is. Imagine if this divine, sacrificial sort of love existed between all the church leaders and members in your area. When Christians begin to treat each other as Paul describes, the world will see and hear the right message. Our unity will attract them, not to us, but to Jesus who is "the way and the truth and the life" (John 14:6).

I know that in pursuing unity God's people face major challenges. The history of the Church is littered with the carnage of destructive and divisive differences, but we cannot allow the past to cloud our vision for the future. We must understand the times in which *we* live. In our individualistic, postmodern society, Christian unity reflects God's selfless love to an increasingly selfish world. We cannot continue to ignore the deep desire of God's heart to bless us and the world around us through the reconciliation of His people.

ENDNOTES

1. Paul E. Billheimer, *Love Covers: A Viable Platform for Christian Unity* (Fort Washington, PA: Christian Literature Crusade Inc., 1981), 7.

2. Edgar J. Goodspeed, *The New Testament: An American Translation* (Chicago, IL: University of Chicago Press, 1923).

3. Mladen Jovanovic, "The Evangelical Perspective on Unity and the Contribution of the Protestant Evangelical Council to Christian Fellowship," *KAIROS: Evangelical Journal of Theology* 2, no. 1 (2008), 79-90.

4. Charles Colson and Ellen Vaughn, *Being the Body* (Nashville, TN: W Publishing, Thomas Nelson, 2003).

CHAPTER 2

THE ANOINTING OIL

—Mark Twain, American author, 1835–1910,
in *Advice to the Unreliable on Churchgoing*, April 12, 1863

At the end of the nineteenth century, when Mark Twain was writing, the prevailing social mores demanded adherence to a conservative, unobtrusive lifestyle, particularly in church. These days, we have to balance an even more complex variety of social, political, and economic conventions with our individual interests. But a concern for the effect our way of life has on those around us remains just as relevant, not only in church services. In contrast to the perfume which Twain could not overlook, the unity of believers should create a pleasing, distinctive impression. In Psalm 133:1-2 we read,

How good and pleasant it is when brothers live together in unity! It is like precious oil poured on the head, running

29

down on the beard, running down on Aaron's beard, down upon the collar of his robes.

This is a beautiful description of unity drawn from the inauguration rites for Aaron as the high priest. We read about it in Leviticus 8. This was a very solemn occasion, a onetime event at the start of the nation of Israel. Aaron and his sons were to serve as priests in the newly built Tent of Meeting. When they had ceremonially washed, put on elaborate, clean priestly clothes, and Moses had consecrated ("set apart") the utensils and dedicated the Tent of Meeting, Aaron and his sons were anointed with special oil that gave off a distinctive fragrance.

THE FRAGRANCE OF UNITY

Perfume or aftershave is not something everybody goes for. Scent is a very individual, personal matter. But, like clothes, perfume often seems to sell best when advertised by the name of a current celebrity. Perhaps there is an unconscious desire to be associated with the stinking rich!

In ancient Israel there was one perfume, though, that did not need outrageous advertising superlatives. This unique and heavenly fragrance was intentionally and unmistakeably associated with the God of Israel. It was certainly not for sale. It existed exclusively for the anointing of the priests, was prescribed by God, and made by master perfumers. The carefully selected ingredients combined together to give off a totally unique aroma (see Exod. 30:22-33). Outside the Tent of Meeting, the use of this perfume was forbidden. After the ceremony, with the rich oil dripping down their heads and onto their collars, Aaron and his sons smelled like no one else on earth!

It is this very special perfumed oil which David, in Psalm 133, equates with brothers living together in unity. He emphasizes that the fragrance of unity too is distinct and unique—it is the aroma of the presence of God. We, as Christians, are called to be the "aroma of Christ" to the world around us (2 Cor. 2:15). It is our unity, our mutual love for Jesus and one another that creates this unforgettable fragrance—not just our personal walk with the Lord. Division, on the other hand, is the enemy's trademark, and it stinks.

There is an interesting account in the Bible of King David sending messengers to Hanun, king of the Ammonites, to offer condolences on the death of his father, a friend of David's. Hanun's advisors suspect trickery, so they shave the messengers' beards off and cut up their clothes. We read that the Ammonites, as a result of destroying the friendship between the two nations, figuratively become an offensive smell to David (see 1 Chron. 19:6). Pungent divisiveness also is quickly recognized as cheap and nasty, especially when it is directed toward other believers.

Perfume often evokes memories of past friends who used the same scent. What memories and impressions do we evoke among our friends and acquaintances? Is it the aroma of unity with Christ or something less pleasant? A prayer spoken for the need of a fellow Christian, an encouraging sentence to a believing colleague, or an act of practical kindness to a neighbor can spread a much more noticeable fragrance than the perfume we spray on our neck each morning.

UNITY STARTS WITH THE HEAD

The anointing oil was poured onto the head of the priest and then ran down over his beard and onto his robe. Some consider Aaron's name to mean "mountainous" or "mountain of strength," providing an obvious parallel with Mount Hermon which David mentions later in Psalm 133. The whole psalm appears to hinge on the idea of unity summed up in the representative role of the high priest, the "man at the top." Blessing is to be found in unity—from top to toe or mountaintop to valley. All of Israel would be blessed by unity, from the highest to the lowest. All will be brothers.

In extending this illustration to the Church, it is axiomatic that Christ is the Head of the Church, His Body. Through Him we are cleansed and anointed by the Holy Spirit, as explained by Paul to the Ephesians (see Eph. 5:23-27). Our spiritual relationship is first and foremost with Jesus, the Son of God. Only through our personal relationship with Him are we related to our fellow brothers and sisters. However, in the same letter, Paul points out that the leaders in the church (apostles, prophets, evangelists, pastors, and teachers) have been given by God "so that the body of Christ may be built up until we all reach unity in the faith" (see Eph. 4:11-13). In other words, the blessing of unity starts when the leaders, anointed by the Holy Spirit for their ministry, allow the blessing to flow down to others. As members of local and regional churches, one of our most important responsibilities is to pray for our leaders so that they can set an example in their contacts with each other.

Qualifications for Leadership

In many churches today there seems to be an overemphasis on intellectual qualifications for spiritual leadership. The more degrees studied, the better the minister! I am not devaluing such qualifications per se. I have several degrees myself (though not in theology). For Paul, all his qualifications were irrelevant; in his own words, he "considered them rubbish." It was his relationship with Christ alone that gave him the right to stand before God (see Phil. 3:8-9). His greatest desire was to introduce others to Jesus, serving "with [his] whole heart in preaching the gospel" (Rom. 1:9). He saw his major role as a matchmaker, bringing people in contact with Jesus and encouraging those who already knew Him to develop their relationship with Him and each other more deeply. These are the qualities that set Paul apart as a leader, and they are just as essential today.

In his letter to the Ephesians, Paul was not writing to a single local church. He was writing to *the* Church in that city. Ephesus was a colorful, multicultural city. The Christians there came from a variety of different religious backgrounds and nationalities. The message had to be preached citywide until "all [God's people] reach unity in the faith...attaining to the whole measure of the fullness of Christ" (Eph. 4:13). To represent Jesus adequately they needed each other; the leaders in Ephesus were called upon to make this clear.

In the face of the stressful, fast-paced life many have to deal with today, this supportive unity among church leaders surely has never been more important. A network of mutual relationships would seem to be an existential priority. Yet, in many places the picture is very different. In Proverbs, we read that "an offended brother is more unyielding than a fortified city, and disputes are like the barred gates of a citadel" (Prov. 18:19). It is so disheartening when church leaders, rather than addressing disputes and differences, lock themselves in their castles, letting only the like-minded in. Again, as church members we can play a role in restoring links. When members of different denominational groups start meeting socially, it may not take long for the leaders to let down the drawbridges of love and forgiveness.

Are Denominations Divisive?

The autobiography of the Chinese Christian leader, Brother Yun, *The Heavenly Man,* provides invaluable insight into the outworking of denominational emphases among leaders. Yun tells how God called him as a young man in a Chinese country village to become an evangelist to his atheistic communist country. He records how many people turned to the Lord, but also tells of persecution, torture, and imprisonment. He was a great example to Christians in the Chinese underground house churches, and during the 1970s, at a time of intense persecution, he built up close relationships with other spiritual leaders. Their shared suffering welded them together in a single house church movement.[1]

In the 1980s, the country began to open to international trade, and foreign Christians came, wanting to help the Chinese church. The Bibles they brought were welcome, as these had been precious rarities. But Brother Yun says that the missionary organizations later started sending other books containing materials on denominational theology, ways to worship, and the role of women. Funding was selective, the churches split up, and new movements were formed. The result was that leaders felt unable to walk in unity as this might compromise their new beliefs.[2]

Were the missionaries wrong to distribute their material? Could the Chinese have prevented the new ideas from driving them apart? Was selective denominational funding the cause of the problem? Over the years, I have met, prayed with, worshiped, and worked together with many missionaries. A frequently recurring theme has been their desire to be flexible in the field, remaining open to the Holy Spirit's leading. Yet back home, the mission administration is often too demanding in the requirements it places on its missionaries. Has the Church in the West been exporting sectarianism and legalism at the same time as preaching the Gospel? I would love to see missionary societies adapt their strategies to the local spiritual and cultural needs. For instance, is it really necessary for the local missionary to slight his host's traditionally hospitable offer of a glass of wine just because the society giving his salary requires this? Flexibility in local application of the Gospel could win many more to Christ.

Fortunately, the story does not end there. Brother Yun could not stand idly by and watch the Chinese Church fall apart, so he sought to restore the broken unity.[3] He visited, talked, and prayed with other leaders who had separated. And with tears and hours of difficult discussions, the Lord used him to reconcile many of these leaders, who expressed their desire to learn from one another again.[4] As a result, in the year 2000, the united leaders represented a combined total of 58 million believers! I pray that Christian leaders in Croatia, across Europe, and in other continents will follow the example of the Chinese church and learn from one another, striving to maintain their relationships. Wisdom is needed to distinguish between what is essential and what is not! The Church needs leaders anointed with spiritual discernment.

Unity and Ecumenism

We *must* pray for our leaders. God sees their hearts and knows whether they are willing to love one another and work together. Maintaining unity is much more important to Him than taking a stand on doctrines which may not be fundamental for salvation. Besides, spiritual unity is not the same as ecumenism (the search for agreement between denominations and confessions) or shared membership in a particular denomination. Apart from Jesus, no human being is perfect (see Rom. 3:23), and certainly no human institution, full of imperfect human beings, can adequately embody the Church as a whole. Christian unity is only possible among people who have been adopted or baptized by confessed faith in the saving blood of Jesus into the spiritual family of God. It is the inevitable outworking of the creative love of the Holy Spirit in individual lives. I have my doubts about the outcome of prolonged discussions by institutional leaders seeking to reconcile contrasting denominational theology. The risk of this sort of ecumenism is that it can take us down two alternative dead-end roads. The one can broaden into an attempt to persuade the other party to come around to my way of thinking. The second path can become so vague and unprincipled that there is neither anything left to disagree about nor any basis for belief. Finding ways to reconcile our differences, including doctrinal standpoints, is of course crucial when we have a shared goal or ministry. But we are not united through shared doctrines—only by faith in the blood of Jesus and the power of the Holy Spirit—in spite of our differences!

Here, it should be mentioned that the Second Vatican Council (Vatican II, 1962–1965, called by Pope John XXIII) at which, among many other issues, the importance of unity, common worship, and cooperation was expressed, undoubtedly changed the stance of the Roman Catholic church. As a result of the encouragement to dialogue with "separated brethren" in other denominations (continued by Popes John Paul II and Benedict XVI), there has been greater opportunity for contacts and fellowship, not least through ecumenical communities and the Catholic Charismatic Renewal movement. Although the Council decrees also reinforce the traditional doctrinal differences, my own experience is that there is much to be gained by developing personal contacts with Roman Catholic believers, particularly when they are based on a common practical or community-orientated goal.

God uses innumerable ways to bring people into a relationship with Jesus and to fill them with His Spirit. But, too often, we put more store by the means to achieve it than the evidence of that relationship in believers' lives. The fruit of the Spirit is confirmation of whether we are true disciples or not. Love, joy, peace, patience, kindness, goodness, faithfulness, and self-control (see Gal. 5:22) cannot be achieved by discussions between religious institutions or their representatives. Unity on this level is supernatural. It is the inevitable outworking of God's love in individual lives.

I urge leaders to give prayerful consideration to the central importance of Christian unity. As we shall see later, unity grows as we walk together in agreement—or at least as we agree to walk together (see Amos 3:3). Time and commitment are needed to allow the relationships to grow, and they become deeper when we are walking together in a shared activity or interest. However, it is easy to build a friendship when we are in agreement on key issues; maturity enables us to build the relationship when we agree to differ.

Just think of the spiritual impact we can make if a thousand Christians start to coordinate their activities instead of each group trying to raise support for themselves. What if in each neighborhood across our cities, leaders started encouraging their members to care for one another, intentionally seeking out fellow believers, helping one another, irrespective of local church allegiances? It is not in our Sunday services that the world sees Jesus; it is in our everyday lives and relationships.

Unity Is an Expression of Maturity

Our unity, like the oil of anointing, flows from the head down over the beard (see Ps. 133:2). This is a physical sign, even today in Middle Eastern countries, of adult manhood and maturity. Maintaining unity in the face of differences of opinion, alternative ways of looking at a situation, and varying tastes or traditions requires spiritual maturity. Children tend to scream or hit out if they cannot get what they want. They usually have to be taught how to get on with one another. For Paul, quarreling and jealousy were signs of spiritual infancy, of a church that had not grown up (see 1 Cor. 3:1-3). We may have reasonable harmony within our own local denominational church, but if we are at loggerheads with other churches in the city, then we are not spiritually mature, whatever spiritual gifts may be in use in our services! Perhaps most of us are less mature than we think!

Respect as a Sign of Maturity

There is no problem in disagreeing with one another. No one has the full picture. But we have to be careful not to consider all our own opinions and attitudes as necessarily better than those of another believer. As with the critics of Peter's visit to Cornelius (see Acts 11:2-3), our disapproval can easily reflect a lack of understanding of God's strategy. Sometimes our zeal for "the Truth"—wanting to "put the other person right"—has more to do with our personal background and experience than eternal principles. Consequently, maturity is measurable in terms of openness, active listening, understanding, and graciousness, rather than pushing a subjective point of view.

In challenging the Philippian believers to be like-minded and united in spirit and purpose, Paul appeals to them "in humility [to] consider others better than yourselves" (Phil. 2:3). The value of this advice is supported by Jim C. Collins, an international management expert, who found in a research study that the most reproducible characteristic of great business leaders is humility.[5] We have to be on the lookout for incipient pride. My own experience in church and secular life is that my ego and self-satisfaction are strengthened by people who agree with me. On the other hand, I benefit more from those who have the courage and friendliness to openly listen to and challenge me. Differing standpoints can be positive when constructively shared.

Even if we do agree to disagree, this is not a reason to become emotional, slandering and ridiculing the other, but to accept that our fellow believers have a right to their opinions and to respect them. After all, self-control is a mature fruit of the Holy Spirit. In the face of disagreement, we should still look for what we appreciate and can encourage in one another, rather than using our differences as a basis for criticism (see also Chapter 6).

In his challenging book *Love Covers,* Paul E. Billheimer, then already well into his eighties, questions,

> Are we sufficiently mature in agape love to accept those whom He [God] accepts? Or are we so egotistical that our opinion in nonessentials is more important to us than unity with God's family and ours? Are we more interested in maintaining our point of view than in helping to bring unity within Christ's Body?[6]

Are we willing to resist the urge to defend our standpoint? We all have something to hide—a weakness, failure, habit, or tendency. It helps to have this in mind when faced with differences between Christians. By mutually respecting our distinct views, we may find that we can strengthen each other in less controversial areas.

Paul states that the Church becomes mature when we "reach unity in the faith" (see Eph. 4:11-13). Many Western Christians, full of theology, doctrines, and tradition, think we have the most mature Christianity. But we often reveal our childishness in our quarreling, bickering, divisions, and petty criticisms. Bill Johnson, pastor of Bethel Church, Redding, California, in a recent sermon, succinctly stated that unity is not a question of agreement, but a matter of being family.[7] Disagreements can be accommodated in a loving family. We do not necessarily need more conferences on areas of theological agreement, but we do need more fathers in the faith who courageously wear the spiritual "beard" of loving maturity and family unity. It is when we leave our doctrinal high ground and put our faith into practice in supporting, caring, and meeting needs throughout the relational family of God that our maturity becomes apparent.

Maintaining Unity When Directions Differ

Even when believers recognize and share this spiritual family relationship, differences in vision or practice among the members may lead some to pursue divergent goals. But this should not undermine our basic unity.

Years ago, when living in Germany, we regularly attended a Baptist church in the east of the city. A group of us had to travel from homes in the north and were keen to start a new fellowship group there. Since we got on well together, we assumed—without specific discussion—that we shared the same goals. So Elaine and I rented a bungalow, and with the help of the church members, we set up a room in our cellar to hold services. These were initially great times. But gradually we realized our expectations did not square with those of the others. We had good friendships, but differed in matters of faith and spiritual gifts. It was difficult to find a common direction. One Sunday, after much prayer and heart-searching, we announced that we were leaving the fellowship—even though it met in our house!

God provided accommodation, and within three days the others had found another room to rent. Elaine and I did not want to depart in acrimony, so we simply left, without trying to justify our decision. Importantly, a year or so later, we came into contact again with members of the still flourishing Baptist church and explained our move more thoroughly, and the lines of communication remain open today. I thank God that this was possible, as we were able to disagree in love but still maintain our family unity in the Lord.

Paul and Barnabas also had at least two disagreements, one about Jews eating with Gentiles (see Gal. 2:13) and another about whether to take Barnabas' cousin, Mark, with them on a return visit to the churches they had established together (see Acts 15:36-41). On the latter issue—said to have been an extremely sharp disagreement—they parted company to visit churches in different countries. But Paul later was respectful when he gave Barnabas full acknowledgment for their joint activities (see Gal. 2:1-10). And Mark was later to be a welcome visitor during Paul's imprisonment, presumably in Rome (see Col. 4:10). Since Paul here clearly recognized Mark as Barnabas' relative, we can assume that Paul and Barnabas were still in contact. So Paul practiced what he preached! He maintained contact, respect, and unity with his fellow believers, even after disagreements. If God is moving us in a different direction from that of other believers and Christian groups, we do not have to force ourselves to stay together, but we should at least keep the lines of communication open and free of bitterness. Spiritual maturity gives us the ability to maintain respect and openness. This is the way of love.

UNITY AFFECTS HOW WE ACT

The anointing oil was said by David to flow from the priest's beard down onto his robe (see Ps. 133:2). In this way, the expensive, jewel-encrusted linen clothes—specially prepared for the priests to be worn during their activities in the Tent of Meeting—were also sanctified (see Lev. 8:7-9,30).

Clothes make a strong impression on the onlooker. I am fascinated by fashion and have acted several times as an informal shopping advisor to friends seeking to change their image. We can appear elegant, sexy, slovenly, or professional, depending on what we wear. The Bible says quite a lot about clothing, describing in detail the various garments that were worn by the priests. But we are also informed how the Church, the Bride of Christ, should be dressed. Paul writes that "you who were baptised into Christ have clothed yourselves with Christ" (Gal. 3:27). When we commit our lives to Him, we are now baptized into and clothed with the nature of Christ. In this way, we freely receive interwoven garments of salvation, righteousness, and praise (see Isa. 61:3,10).

The Robe of Righteousness

The concept of being clothed with righteousness through faith in Christ is taken up several times in Paul's letters (see Eph. 4:24; Phil. 3:19). It contrasts starkly with the state of unredeemed sinners who are described as "unclean, and [whose] righteous acts are like filthy rags" (Isa. 64:6). Without Christ, everything we do for Him is dirty and unacceptable to God, no better than nakedness. An allegory of His cleansing work of salvation is given in Zechariah chapter 3, where the previously filthy garments of self-unrighteousness worn by the high priest Joshua are removed and replaced with clean expensive priestly garments. Jesus has done the same for us as believers in making us a royal priesthood (see 1 Pet. 2:9). The righteousness we receive is "from God and is by faith" (Phil. 3:9).

Unlike designer clothes, we do not have to pay for God's spiritual textiles. But whatever we do, as redeemed priests of God, is only acceptable to Him when we do it trusting in the strength and capability that God has freely given us. The Bible makes it clear that our acts are righteous not because of *what* we do, but because of *why* we do them. Righteous acts are those carried out in faith for the glory of God and the extension of His Kingdom. This applies to individuals and churches. Anything we do that is not by faith is not acceptable to God (see Rom. 14:23). We see an illustration of this very early after the ritual of the anointing of the Aaronic priests had been initiated. Two of Aaron's sons decided they were going to offer sacrifices in their own way. As a result, they immediately died (see Lev. 10:1-2).

After Pentecost, the immediate death of Ananias and Sapphira must have had as dramatic an effect on the new Christians in Jerusalem as the death of Aaron's sons had on the young nation of Israel (see Acts 5:1-11). They tried to do things for their own benefit and to cheat God. His response was similar in both cases: "There is a right or righteous way, and if you do things the wrong way, it is going to have unpleasant effects." (See Matthew 6:1.) This is relevant both for individuals and groups of Christians. Thank God He does not always deal with us based on what we do wrong, but on the basis of His mercy.

Behavior in Keeping With Our Clothing

Many Christians have strong views about the right way to dress. The generation gap and changing fashions certainly leave plenty of room for criticism of modern styles. Christians also should have a "style," but not one that is connected to the latest fashion. God's robes come in all shapes and sizes, depending on the location. We should not judge others by the length of our hems, either in textile or in the text of the Law.

However, since we are clothed in Christ's righteousness, our behavior should reflect the way we are "dressed." A doctor will be expected to act in accordance with her white-coated appearance and a military officer in keeping with his uniform. For the Christian, righteous clothes of various hues have been provided by God, not as a result of any personal "qualifications" we have achieved. This is specifically spelled out in Revelation 19:8, where the Bride, the Church, is given fine linen to wear that "stands for the righteous acts of the saints."

Notice that the fine linen represents the righteousness acts of *all* the saints, the whole Bride of Christ. This is where unity comes in. Led by the Holy Spirit, our combined actions should be directed toward the Kingdom of God (see Matt. 6:33), building up the whole Body of Christ (see Eph. 4:16). Each of us has a role to play, but we are in this together! Like the horse in a pantomime, we share the same costume, but the front needs to be coordinated with the back so that we function properly. We do not necessarily need to put on interdenominational pantomimes, but celebration events like those organized by Hillsong, Soul Survivor, or Spring Harvest to get young people energized for a life of worship are wonderful denominational barrier breakers.

As with Aaron, the fine linen garment of righteousness actually forms part of our spiritual underwear, reflecting our underlying desires and motivations. If we are not acting in faith and trust in the righteousness we have received from Christ and a desire to be a blessing to others, but out of our own conviction or selfish ambition, then we are wearing dirty underclothes!

Just look at the letter to Laodicea in Revelation chapter 3. God accuses the church in Laodicea of being lukewarm, indolent, self-sufficient, and indifferent to God's help. They were trusting in their own righteousness! God points out their real condition: "You are wretched, pitiful, poor, blind and naked. I counsel you to buy from Me...white clothes to wear, so that you can cover your shameful nakedness" (Rev. 3:17-18). Like the emperor in Grimm's famous fairy tale, the Laodiceans, proud of their self-righteousness, considered themselves to be reflecting beautiful religious piety, when in fact they were naked and repulsive.

Laodicea is undoubtedly an accurate description of some churches in the West today. With a comfortable lifestyle and a good-sized congregation, the established traditions of the denomination, and a building in a middle-class neighborhood, the Church is no longer burning with evangelistic fervor. Contact with an inner-city church, where down-and-outs and drug addicts are regular attendees, is unthinkable! As individuals and as members of a church community, we cannot afford to overlook the fact that our robe of righteousness is shared among us. It is to be kept clean by the washing powder of God's Word and softened by the fluid of humility. There is no better way of being kept humble than to serve and share with other Christians, open to their advice and correction.

The Overcoat of Love

Satisfied with their own "appearance," the Laodiceans failed to realize that their final, outermost piece of clothing was missing: "And over all these virtues put on love, which binds them all together in perfect unity" (Col. 3:14). Love for the Lord and for one another is the crucial garment that binds us together in unity. This is the coat by which we are most immediately recognized, the cord that draws all the others together, the outfit which demonstrates the family to which we belong, and the indicator of our commitment to the Body of Christ. Love "is not proud...it is not self-seeking" (1 Cor. 13:4-5), so by putting on love we also follow Peter's advice to "clothe yourselves with humility toward one another" (1 Pet. 5:5).

It is this outer robe of love, anointed by the oil of unity that David talks about in Psalm 133:2. The oil soaks into the collar of the robe and adds its special fragrance to the clothing. Drawing closer together in unity—sharing, encouraging, and working with one another—our love deepens and grows for one another and for the Lord. This is what Paul describes in First Corinthians 13—not just the love of the Lord we experience as individual believers, but the love of Christ flowing through all our relationships binding us together as one Body in Him.

I have worked together with some gracious Roman Catholic colleagues and had great fun and fellowship with radical Charismatics and hospitable Plymouth Brethren. I have enjoyed times of prayer with Roman Catholic, Pentecostal, Reformed, Methodist, and Baptist believers. These have been people from all walks of life and from countries on every one of the five continents, and our lives are richer as a result. God's love shared together is wonderful, and too many Christians are simply missing out. They are naked and do not realize it!

Supporting the Family

We all come from different backgrounds and families. I and my wife Elaine have never ceased to be thankful that we both grew up in families with long-standing, loving Christian traditions. Over the years, we have had many opportunities to help and encourage those less fortunate, who have grown up in broken or dysfunctional families. Deep down inside, each one of us wants to be part of a loving, supportive family that gives us a solid basis for learning, working and pursuing our goals. This is what God has planned for all of us. He has created not just the individual nuclear families, but wants us to explore the richness, diversity, and encouragement of the wider family. I have a small family circle, so I really appreciate my second cousins in Vancouver, Canada, who we get to see from time to time. Living by ourselves in Central and Eastern Europe, it is always a joy to visit parents, brothers, sisters, and children back in the UK. But a close, loving family also provides opportunity to be of assistance ourselves. Elaine found this recently in caring for my mother in the UK after an operation and in supporting her aunt in South Africa when her husband died. This is what God is offering to each of us—a diverse, loving, supportive family to which we can contribute—if we are willing to look beyond the walls of religious restrictions we have built around ourselves.

How can we each help to sustain the unity of God's family? Of course, we have responsibilities toward our physical families and local church communities. But God wants His aroma of love to spread much wider. It is mainly a question of finding the common denominators, often of a rather mundane nature. Are there people who appear to be Christians in our place of work? Why not get to know them and start encouraging and supporting one another in a professional capacity? Do you like sports? How about trying to set up a local sports league with teams from different churches? We did this with football teams in the UK, Germany and Croatia, and several unbelievers, including one of the current youth leaders of the Baptist church in Zagreb, became Christians as a result of playing on our teams. When did you last invite a neighbor to your home for coffee? Are there elderly people in the neighborhood who could be cared for by Christians from different backgrounds? The possibilities are endless. We just have to take the first steps in building the relationships.

ENDNOTES

1. Brother Yun and Paul Hattaway, *The Heavenly Man* (London, UK: Monarch Books, 2002), 232.

2. Yun and Hattaway, *The Heavenly Man*, 234.

3. Yun and Hattaway, *The Heavenly Man*, 235.

4. Yun and Hattaway, *The Heavenly Man*, 240.

5. Jim C. Collins in a lecture to the 2010 Willow Creek Global Leadership Summit, available from http://www.willowcreek.com/wca_prodsb.asp?invtid=PR34744.

6. Paul E. Billheimer, *Love Covers*, 66.

7. Bill Johnson, "Gathering Around Fathers," http://www.youtube.com/watch?v=6CGIUdjD0eE (last viewed Nov. 3, 2011).

CHAPTER 3

THE REFRESHING DEW

WATER IS LIFE'S MATER AND MATRIX, MOTHER AND MEDIUM.
THERE IS NO LIFE WITHOUT WATER.

—Albert Szent-Györgyi, Hungarian biochemist,
1893-1986, Nobel Prize winner, 1937

Many years ago I spent a couple of weeks on a research project at the Hadassah Medical Center in the Hebrew University of Jerusalem. South of the city, the ground was dry, desolate desert, even in November. But as we drove north one day to the Sea of Galilee, we passed plantations of tall bananas, olive groves, and other healthy-looking plants irrigated by the water from the Jordan River. This river is formed by four tributaries that collect water from the slopes of Mount Hermon. It then flows through Lake Hula, before draining down through the Sea of Galilee and the Jordan Valley to evaporate in the heat of the Dead Sea. The river is the major source of fresh water for the whole country. The source of this vital aquatic lifeline is Mount Hermon, a 2814 meters (9232 feet) high mountain to the north of Israel, often covered in snow in winter, and frequently watered by clouds (with an annual rainfall of 1100–1300 millimeters; 43–51 inches) which feed the river.

47

Irrigating Water

In Psalm 133, David likens brothers living together in unity to the life-giving water falling on Mount Hermon: "It is as if the dew of Hermon were falling on Mount Zion" (Ps. 133:3). Zion was the ancient Jebusite fortress conquered by David that later became the site of Solomon's temple inside the city of Jerusalem. In contrast to its northern counterpart, Mount Zion is much smaller, at about 760 meters (2493 feet), with an annual rainfall of 660 millimeters (26 inches). In the summer months from June to September there is practically no rain, and a scorching desert wind, the *sharav*, bakes the city. If the same "dew" that falls on Mount Hermon were to fall on Mount Zion, particularly in summer, the climate would be transformed! Most of King David's people lived around Mount Zion. So David was saying that when people live together in unity it is as though all the refreshing water that flows from Mount Hermon, providing life to the land, were giving life and strength just to those in Jerusalem and Judah.

Unity Brings Enjoyment

Brothers living together in unity give joy, life, growth, and refreshment to themselves and others with whom they come into contact. A similar sentiment is expressed in Psalm 84. The songwriter describes a group of travelers jointly trusting the Lord as they make a pilgrimage to Zion: "As they pass through the Valley of Baca, they make it a place of springs" (Ps. 84:6). Baca, a waterless desert, is changed to a place of springs and rainfall as this joyful group passes through, going "from strength to strength" (Ps. 84:7). When Christians are working together with vision and a passion for the Lord and the Church, we have an inevitably positive effect on our immediate environment.

Often we become so preoccupied with work and the pursuit of prosperity we forget that God does not want our lives to consist of drudgery and obligations. Jesus said that He came to give us life "to the full" (John 10:10). One of the greatest incentives to closer practical unity with other Christians is that life becomes more enjoyable! We can be much more productive, both materially and spiritually, when we share our capabilities, working in concert. Bearing in mind that the Body of Christ should be clothed in righteousness and love, listen to what Solomon, the wisest ruler ever, writes, "He who pursues righteousness and love finds life, prosperity and honor" (Prov. 21:21). Living together in unity is fun as well! Personally, I gain more enjoyment from a barbecue with a cross section of fellow believers than listening to the backbiting at a secular cocktail party.

The Irrigation Must Be Sustained

My best friends are those with whom I have a long history. Our oldest friends date back to the years when Elaine and I were students. These are people with whom we talked into the night, went on journeys, prayed, and played sports. My friend Mike and I hitchhiked the length of England, from London to Newcastle and back as students—just for the weekend! We know all about each other—our strengths, weaknesses, and failures. And even though we live thousands of miles apart, each time we meet, it is as though the last meeting was only yesterday. With other friends, Elaine and I have shared holidays, church fellowships, tears, joys, and visions. Some acquaintances could perhaps have developed into closer relationships, but our jobs, families, church commitments, or even the language barrier made this difficult. Relationships of any kind need time to develop. This applies both to our personal relationship with the Lord and to our involvement with one another.

The snow, rain, or dew falling on Mount Hermon only makes the surrounding land fertile because it receives regular precipitation. If rain falls once every few years in the desert, some of the dormant seeds will spring to life and give a quick blaze of colorful flowers. Seen on BBC television documentaries with time-lapse photography, this is truly amazing. But the desert dryness quickly returns. Unless we make a priority of maintaining the unity that Christ has given us, any infrequent contacts are going to be just flashes in the pan. If our love for the Lord and one another is weak, the spiritual blessing we are looking for will be transient. As God said through the prophet Hosea, "Your love is like the morning mist, like the early dew that disappears" (Hos. 6:4-5). Without repeated irrigation of our relationships with care, love, and attention, the unity that cost Jesus so much to achieve will wilt and fade.

Some people are more task-orientated, and few of us are able to find as much time for each other as we should like. I think the practical approach is to plant the roots deep early on. Deep roots help the plant to resist dry periods better. I am still good friends with Mike because we got to know each other well at the beginning, so the relationship can withstand the long gaps when we are not in contact. The secret is to give individuals the attention they deserve, right from the start—even if the contact is relatively short. I am always impressed by some U.S. friends who, when meeting someone for the first time, repeat back in greeting the name of the person to whom they have just been introduced.

"I'm Jack."

"Oh! Hello, Jack. Pleased to meet you."

This interest and attention can be continued during the ensuing conversation. As a task-orientated person myself, I still have a lot to learn about this.

Once we have made a good contact, the same attentive regard for the individual is required. I found, when our children were young, that it was not necessary to plan an hour a day with them—it usually did not fit in with their play schedule! Much more effective was to stop what I was doing and give my son or daughter 30 seconds of complete attention. That was usually sufficient before they ran off to their friends again. Fruitful time is not necessarily long, but selflessly offered.

To strengthen relationships we also have to be prepared to overlook and forgive minor irritations and to talk through potentially contentious issues. By showing consideration and forgiveness toward abrasive colleagues, with time, even critics can be won over as friends.

We have developed good relationships with fellow Christians in several different churches across Zagreb. We have prayed together regularly, spent time walking in the parks and countryside, eaten together, talked, and shared our concerns. A group of international Christian women from several continents and one special, hospitable family of believers have been very encouraging in this respect, organizing events and meetings in their homes. Not everyone has the same amount of time, but it is what we do with the time we have that counts! Despite our differences, we have got to know and love one another, even with busy lifestyles. This gives new strength to our resolve to reach the whole city for the Kingdom of God. We are in this together, and the task becomes lighter as the burden is shared.

REAPING THE HARVEST

God wants to "make rivers flow on barren heights and springs within the valleys" (Isa. 41:18). Our cities and towns are in great need of spiritual renewal. We should all make it a high priority to pray for God to send His rain of blessing and revival on the dry ground of human hearts (see Deut. 11:14; Joel 2:23; Zech. 10:1; James 5:7). It is not Zagreb alone that needs justice to "roll on like a river, [and] righteousness like a never-failing stream" (Amos 5:24). Across the world, economies are reeling under the effects of uncontrolled personal greed. Respect, mercy, consideration, and the traditional standards of fairness and justice appear to have been thrown out the windows of the many tall skyscrapers of aggressive businesses. Now more than ever, it is time for the Church of God to set an example to the urban community. As God's people, we bear responsibility not only toward our Father in Heaven, but also for the eternal destiny of the people around us. We are the channels through whom God will pour His streams of justice, righteousness, and revival.

We are also responsible for breaking up the soil so that righteousness can be sown (see Hos. 10:12). Rather than wielding our doctrinal and interpersonal differences as weapons, let us "beat [our] swords into ploughshares" (Isa. 2:4) to break up the dry, hard hearts of our neighbors and colleagues with fervent prayer. This will prepare the ground for the "autumn rains in righteousness" (Joel 2:23-24) that God has promised to send so that the harvest is substantial.

Harvesting From a Desert

For many years, the small local churches in my hometown on the southwest coast of England kept themselves more-or-less to themselves. Despite regular evangelistic missions to the crowded beaches in the summers, the churches, composed mainly of older people, struggled to survive. The Congregational church closed down many years ago and became a fossil museum. The Baptist church was rocked by division and hounded-out the pastor. For decades, the Brethren fellowship rarely consisted of double-digit congregations. And the Anglican Parish church became little more than a social club, the vicar usually more drunk on wine than on the Holy Spirit. But there were a few faithful Christians who kept believing and praying and encouraging one another.

In recent years, other believers moved into the area, among them a middle-aged couple who joined the Anglican church. They challenged the spiritual credentials of the vicar and asked the Archbishop to appoint a vicar who was a true believer, rather than just in name. The bishop agreed, and things started to change. Soon Christians from several of the local churches started a joint quarterly meeting in a village hall to pray together for their town.

Within a short time, more than 50 people were meeting to pray. The Brethren fellowship redecorated its nineteenth-century frontage and once a month visited every home on the local housing estates. A recent Christmas carol service there—without the tourists—was attended by 85 people, including supporting believers from other churches, and eight visitors committed their lives to the Lord! No desert is too dry, no waterless place too bleak that it cannot blossom when a united, Spirit-led group of believers works and prays together in commitment to the Lord and to one another.

Do Not Let the Ripe Corn Rot

Jesus said that "the harvest is plentiful but the workers are few" (Matt. 9:37). Unless we start living and working together, the "ripe corn" is going to rot and spoil. I have taken a few business trips to the American Midwest and viewed from the air the prairies containing the vast areas of the Corn Belt. To harvest the ripe corn before the weather breaks, huge armies of combine harvesters work in a coordinated fashion, throughout the day and night, making the most of the warm, dry weather. It would be pointless for individual farmers to go out with their old-fashioned scythes to cut down the rolling fields of corn. They would be exhausted and only harvest a few small shocks of corn. Even with combine harvesters, the work is too much for single machines, working in an uncoordinated way. Too much of the harvest would be lost.

But is not this the approach we as Christians have been taking for decades or even centuries? The wide prairies of white, ripe "corn" stretch out from our doorsteps. Yet we are still hacking, with our archaic scythes of restricted, insular, denominational tradition, at the little bit of corn in front of our noses, expending great time and energy! It makes much better sense—even in terms of human logic—to combine our resources and work together for the harvest of souls! The task is too large to avoid cooperation.

But to address this enhancement of spiritual and evangelistic ergonomics, we have to change our whole attitude. We need to be *actively* looking and praying for people with whom to cooperate. Perhaps this is the crux of the whole matter. Has it ever occurred to us that working together in unity for God's Kingdom is more efficient? And are we willing to make the effort to share the task? The diversity we bring to the task of reaping—as we shall see in the next chapter—is divinely created to allow the work to be shared. We shall not find all the gifts and abilities we need to harvest a whole city just within a single church community.

LIFE FOR EVERMORE

When we are living in unity, dressed in righteousness and love, being refreshed by continual dew and showers, then "the Lord bestows His blessing, even life for evermore" (Ps. 133:3). This happened when Aaron and his sons obeyed God, were anointed, and offered sacrifices as God commanded.

When Moses and Aaron came out of the Tent of Meeting,

> *...they blessed the people; and the glory of the Lord appeared to all the people. Fire came out from the presence of the Lord and consumed the burnt offering...on the altar. And when all the people saw it, they shouted for joy and fell face down* (Leviticus 9:23-24).

The evidence of God's blessing on His people's unity was that His glory was revealed, fire came down from Heaven, and all the people were very happy!

The same sequence of events occurred on the day of Pentecost, when the disciples had "joined together constantly in prayer" (Acts 1:14). Then the Holy Spirit appeared as flames on their heads. Their preaching was powerful; they shared, prayed, and praised together; and people were saved (see Acts 2:42,47). When the Church of God begins to pray, live, and move in unity, the Lord promises that His blessing will be revealed in tangible, physical effects by the power of the life-giving Holy Spirit (see 2 Chron. 7:14; John 16:13; Rom. 8:11).

Encouraging the Ephesians to maintain the unity of the Spirit, Paul prays that they (plural) may be strengthened "with power through His Spirit...according to His power that is work within us, to Him be glory in the church" (Eph. 3:16, 20-21). Our united empowerment by the Holy Spirit is so that the whole Body of Christ can receive the benefit. Aaron and the priests were anointed with oil for service for the whole nation. Water flows down from Mount Hermon to refresh the whole land. So by drawing closer to one another in unity—encouraging, supporting, and strengthening each other—we shall receive an outpouring of God's Holy Spirit for His whole Church.

This is the mystery the Church in the West has failed to grasp; this is the cause of its weakened state; this is the reason we do not see the spiritual breakthroughs for which we have been longing. Instead of drinking from our separately labeled, screw-top bottles of denominationally restricted water, we need to be flowing together as a deep, powerful river of blessing to a dry and thirsty world. This is the key to the Kingdom of Heaven: the whole Church in a community living, working, and praying together, seeking to "keep the unity of the Spirit through the bond of peace" (Eph. 4:3) and acting *together,* as a result, in the fullness and power of the Holy Spirit!

Characterized by Boldness

As the disciples prayed together, shortly after Pentecost, the room was shaken, and they were filled with the Holy Spirit to speak boldly (see Acts 4:31). *Boldness combined with the fruit of the Spirit is the litmus test for the blessing of God on the Church and the indicator of a church moving in unity and authority.* Too often we count the number of people at a church service as the reflection of God's blessing. But how bold and fruitful are those people in their prayer, faith, and expectations? Are we willing to take a stand, speaking and acting unashamedly for the Lord?

Years ago, Elaine and I were on holiday in the Austrian Alps. Being amateur British visitors, we were not exactly professionally equipped in our T-shirts, shorts, and sneakers! As we started up the mountain path, we passed a German family—mother, father, and teenage children all fully equipped with *Lederhosen*, backpacks, red-checked shirts, alpine hats, thick woolen socks, solid walking boots, and sturdy walking sticks. They looked much more the part than we did! A few hours later, tired but highly satisfied at having made the steep climb successfully, Elaine and I reached the summit. And who did we see climbing out of the cable-car, fresh-faced and cheerful? It was the overdressed German family, who despite their appearance, had chosen to take the easy way up! How many of us are like that? We have the right appearance, attend the right services, and say the correct things doctrinally. But the boldness, enthusiasm, and power are missing!

We do not have to wait for our church leaders to tell us what to do. We do not have to ask for permission to tell others about the greatness of our God. We do need, however, to spend time with the Lord. He is the Source of our power and love. Each day, even when I am working on my computer, I try to keep in contact with Him. We need to find out what God wants to do through us and then let Him do it! Ask the Holy Spirit how to build up contacts with your neighbors and colleagues. Ask Him to give you more love for His people, and pray for opportunities to meet other believers who share the same vision of the Church in victory. Our boldness and passion will grow as we allow the Holy Spirit to lead us.

Empowered by the Holy Spirit

When Aaron and his sons were anointed, they also received spiritual power and authority to perform their priestly ministry. Only then were they permitted to offer the sacrifices for the people (see Lev. 9:1-24). Not long before this anointing ceremony, Aaron had made a golden calf as an idol for the people, just because they wanted it. Yet after his anointing, when his sons were killed for incorrectly offering sacrifices to Yahweh, Aaron and his remaining sons boldly stuck to their tasks as priests. They did not even attend the funeral because the anointing was still on them (see Lev. 10:1-7). The Holy Spirit gives us the power to be different, to live in unity, peace, and love with one another. His work in us *together* is the evidence that we are a chosen people so that when an outsider joins us and recognizes the presence of the Spirit, he gives praise to God (see 1 Cor. 14:24-25).

Christian unity is impossible without the Holy Spirit. We are baptized by one Spirit into one Body (see Eph. 4:4-5). Our immersion into the Body of Christ, through faith in what Jesus achieved for us on the cross, is made possible by the Holy Spirit. The specific ministry of a believer within the Church must be mediated by a renewal of power in the Holy Spirit, to strengthen the unity of the Church (see Eph. 4:11-13). The extent to which we "make every effort to keep the unity of the Spirit" (Eph. 4:3) will directly affect the degree of anointing of the Holy Spirit on us. The channels will be open between us, allowing the Holy Spirit to fill us up. As a corollary, the extent to which we fail to recognize or maintain the unity of *all* true believers in a particular location will restrict to the same degree the outworking of the Holy Spirit!

Kenneth Hagin was a Pentecostal preacher and evangelist in the U.S. during the twentieth century. He was something of a controversial figure during his lifetime, but was a great blessing to many people who believed or who were healed as a result of his preaching. In the last few pages of his book *Understanding the Anointing,*[1] he comments on one of the most remarkable periods in his life. This was in 1939–40, when the world was in a state of financial, political, military, and economic upheaval. He was pastoring a church that was so united the Holy Spirit was able to work in a way Hagin had never experienced before or since. The Sunday morning services were attended mainly by believing church members, and the presence of the Holy Spirit was such that often everyone was quiet, in a state of reverence. No one felt the need to take a lead because the Holy Spirit was in control. Repeatedly, unbelievers came into the room and were so challenged by God's presence that they fell down, confessed their sins, and surrendered their lives to the Lord without anyone saying anything. This, I believe, is what can happen anywhere when believers are completely united and share a common desire to glorify God. This is the blessing that God gives to brothers and sisters living together in unity. As Paul E. Billheimer wrote nearly 40 years ago,

> The supreme miracle of unity of the Body would release
> the Holy Spirit in a world-wide revival of the miraculous
> that would dwarf all previous demonstrations and
> usher in an ingathering of souls around the world in

unprecedented proportions. Only the unity of the Body can produce the real "latter rain" for which we pray.[2]

A Spring of Living Water

What can we do? Jesus said that whoever believes in Him will experience such a filling of the Holy Spirit that "streams of living water will flow from within him" (John 7:38). Each of us should be thirsty for the presence and power of the Holy Spirit. Jesus promised that when we are thirsty for more of Him, He will fill us (see Matt. 5:6). When the Holy Spirit starts flowing in our lives, we shall inevitably carry others along with us. In a dry land, water is very much sought after. We only have to start sharing with friends and colleagues what God has been doing in our lives, and others will also want to know more. This can be done in the local church, at work, on the sports team, or down at the pub. As more people respond, why not arrange to meet to talk, pray, and listen to the Spirit? In my son's church in Glasgow, groups get together to ask the Holy Spirit to reveal the sort of people they should be talking to that week. There have been some amazing conversations. A large river is formed by many little tributaries, streams, and brooks. It only takes one spring to get things going.

ENDNOTES

1. Kenneth Hagin, *Understanding the Anointing* (Tulsa, OK: Rhema Bible Church, 1980).

2. Paul E. Billheimer, *Love Covers*, 130.

CHAPTER 4

UNITY IN DIVERSITY

VARIETY'S THE VERY SPICE OF LIFE
THAT GIVES IT ALL ITS FLAVOUR.

—William Cowper,
English poet, 1731–1800

Jack Welch, the acclaimed former chairman and CEO of General Electric, is widely quoted as having said, "Control your destiny or somebody else will."[1] Many people have followed his advice. The result of greedy individuals taking things into their own hands, at least in finance and business, is only too obvious from the 2008 global economic collapse.

Although a modern phenomenon, the root cause of intense individualism can be found before the birth of world civilizations. The first man, Adam, was seduced by the idea that he and his wife could "be like God" and independently determine whether something is good or evil (Gen. 3:5). Today, a higher moral authority continues to be widely rejected. It is "politically incorrect" to tell anyone else what might be good for them, and individualism has become the dominant industrialized cultural standard. Most people live as they please.

59

Taking their cue from the world around us, many Christians have willingly incorporated self-determination, rather than community living, into their lifestyles. In their book, *Breakout,* Mark Stibbe and Andrew Williams point out that personal faith is often confused with individualistic faith so that the need for Christian community is no longer recognized.[2] Do not get me wrong. Hard work, aiming at worthwhile goals, and provision of a comfortable life for our families are all laudable. The principles I have tried to follow in my professional life are the following: aim for the best; make the most of every opportunity; use the time wisely; learn from the past, understand the present, change the future. But I also believe that people matter more than things and that, if you will acknowledge God, He will honor you.

Our personal impact is shaped by the extent to which we live by God's principles. Sadly, too many Christians remain immature, childishly expecting the local fellowship to meet their subjective requirements: "What is in it for me?" As a result, there is a plague of "butterfly Christians," flitting around from church to church to gain some personal "blessing" before moving on to the next "uplifting experience." Commitment and contribution do not seem to play much of a role here. Often these butterflies go one step further, saying, "I do not find the Church relevant to my requirements, so why bother with church and other Christians at all? My faith is a matter between me and God, so leave me alone to sort things out with Him myself." And they give up meeting with other Christians completely.

Avoiding uncomfortable, interpersonal challenges, we have blunted the sharpness of God's Word, weakened the testimony of the Church, and diluted the message of salvation. *In our individualism and criticism, we have shattered our unity, trampled on our love for each other, and lost the power of God for salvation and revival.* We have become blind to the fact that "Christ loved the *church* and gave Himself up for her…to present her to Himself as a radiant *church,* without stain or wrinkle" (Eph. 5:25,27). It is not all about me, my opinions, or my theology. Jesus does not want an immature, selfish baby as a bride!

Jesus did not die on the cross to make a comfortable life for each individual believer, providing for our personal needs, health, and prosperity! He did not rise from the dead to give us strength to get to the top of the promotion ladder. His chief aim was to win a *people* for Himself; to regain a family; and to raise up a body of believers who *together* would give glory to God on earth and be transformed into a beautiful bride for the King of kings! *I am not the master of my destiny. My destiny is to be one with my Master!* God's priority is His plan for the whole Church, and this is what determines His dealings with individuals.

UNITED TO BUILD

Paul, at the end of his life, lost his individual rights, confined to his house in Rome as a prisoner of the Roman authorities. But rather than lamenting his loss, he writes to the Ephesians, encouraging them to use their freedom to live not for themselves, but for Jesus and His Body, the Church: "Make every effort to keep the unity of the Spirit through the bond of peace" (Eph. 4:3). We too should do all we can to protect our oneness in the Spirit.

Guard the Unity of the Spirit

It is not that we have to work at becoming united, since all who personally confess faith in Him are already made one through the death and resurrection of Christ (see Eph. 2:13-15). Irrespective of physical race, culture, natural abilities, religious doctrine, or practice, when through faith we believe, confess, and live in the realization and demonstration that the Holy Spirit is living within each of us, we are one in the Spirit. It is the oneness *of the Spirit* we are to guard. We do not have to agree with our brother on every point, nor share common rites or even theology, but we should avoid grieving the Holy Spirit in His heart.

We must make it our highest priority, our overriding desire, our guiding principle, and deepest passion to maintain unity with our fellow believers, to keep open the lines of communication. Jesus' longing prayer to His

Father as He faced death was that all believers "may be one...just as You are in Me and I am in You" (John 17:21). This is the purpose for which we have been born again; this is the highest calling toward which we should be striving (see Eph. 4:1). Our love for one another is a direct reflection of our love for the Lord Jesus Himself. By working out in practice, here and now, our unity with other members of His Body, Jesus will be revealed in His transfigured glory to the world around us, in full view of the unseen spiritual powers (see Eph. 6:12).

A Single Spiritual Heredity

When we confess our sin, accept that Jesus died for our salvation, and commit our lives in faith to Him, we receive His new life through the Holy Spirit—a spiritual transplant. Our old nature is removed, and we receive the transplanted genes of the family of God, becoming His spiritual children, related to all our brothers and sisters in Christ. The same spiritual inheritance is implanted into each of us, making us one family, "one new quality of humanity" (Eph. 2:15 AMP). We have "one hope...one Lord, one faith, one baptism" (Eph. 4:4-5). However diverse we may be in characteristics, color, or creed, we are born through one Spirit into one Body.

In John's prophetic vision of Heaven, recorded in Revelation, the four living creatures sing the praises of the Lamb, who with His blood "purchased men for God from every tribe and language and people and nation. [He made] them to be a [single] kingdom and priests to serve our God" (Rev. 5:9-10). In other words, whether we fully approve of other groups of Christians or not, we are all members of *one Kingdom*. We shall be working together in eternity on the new earth. So we might as well learn to get on with each other here and now!

Our children have diverse backgrounds, but a common genetic and spiritual heritage. Philip and Joanna were born in the Netherlands and grew up in Germany, so acquired some Germanic habits. Ian and Simon were born in Germany, but spent their teenage years in Croatia and have a more relaxed attitude, in keeping with the Mediterranean approach to life. All of us communicate in English and German—Ian, Phil, and I in Dutch. Ian is the only one to have mastered Croatian. Joanna, Ian, and I are the only ones with a biomedical education. So there are things we mutually understand, some interests we share, and other areas where we cannot understand each other. But our diversity enriches the family as a whole, particularly at annual Christmas reunions. Philip can give us his legal opinion, Joanna useful insight into social issues, Ian the latest research ideas, and Simon is a fountain of knowledge about films. And we never tire of hearing what God is doing in each of our lives. We are spread across the continent, but regularly keep in touch because of family ties. It is deeply satisfying, as parents, to hear that our children communicate with and visit one another, helping out when advice is needed. In some respects, this is how God wants His family to function. He loves us and is delighted when we contact and encourage one another. Despite the geographical, cultural, and doctrinal distance between us, let us keep the lines of communication open and avoid family splits. At the very least, we can tell each other about the good things God is doing for us. Today, with social networks, this becomes even easier. By drawing the various strands together, the diversity of God's family becomes our strength.

Building Together

Nehemiah, a Jewish exile and cupbearer to Artaxerxes, King of Persia, was given permission to return to Israel to rebuild the walls of Jerusalem, torn down many years earlier by the Babylonian invaders. Importantly, he knew he needed a varied team of builders, so he took some with him and recruited local artisans. But when he started building, the local, non-Jewish civil servants, Sanballat and Tobiah, saw this as a challenge to the comfortable and corrupt way of life they had carved out in this backwater of the empire. They used ridicule, derision, subterfuge, aggression, and finally distraction in an attempt to prevent the walls being rebuilt. Nehemiah immediately recognized the enemy's standard procedure to break up his united team. Instead of entering into discussions with them, he prayed to God for strength (see Neh. 4:9; 6:3). What an example! How many of us behave like this? The natural response is to start criticizing, ridiculing, attacking, and judging—either our competitors, colleagues, neighbors, or other groups of Christians. We get distracted from our goal and dragged down to the enemy's level, where he is much more effective than we are!

As a boy I often heard the comment, "the devil finds work for idle hands." *It is frequently the people who are doing the least to help build the Church who are the most vociferous in their criticisms.* If church leaders were able to engage members in constructive work, they would probably waste less time answering all the criticisms leveled against them!

Nehemiah puts everybody to work, each person fully equipped, with their own part of the wall to build (see Neh. 4:13-15). Half are provided with weapons to defend the wall—just as Paul encourages the Ephesians to equip themselves with spiritually defensive armor (see Neh. 4:16; Eph. 6:10-18). The other half get on with the building, but those who carried materials "did their work with one hand and held a weapon in the other, and each of the builders wore his sword at his side as he worked" (Neh. 4:17-18). What a great picture! As Christians, we each stand with a building implement in one hand and the Bible—the "sword of the Spirit"—to defend against the enemy's attacks in the other (see Eph. 6:17). We are all working in concert across our cities to build the Kingdom. How many walls would be built to keep the enemy out, how many temples of praise erected, and how many spiritually "homeless" wanderers given an eternal house to live in if we had this same resolve?

A wide diversity of skills is needed to build the Kingdom. On a building site, construction activities do not all happen at once. The bulldozers come first to dig the foundations, then the cement mixers to fill in the hole. The reinforced concrete walls, drains, and electric connections come next. Later the roofers, plumbers, decorators, and electricians arrive, and eventually the gardener comes to plant the trees and shrubs. The electrician and plumber may never meet the bulldozer driver, but all are in contact with the foreman. They work together on the same project, with the goal of completing the job successfully. In the same way, in the Church, our unity is revealed at various levels. Even if our theology differs, we can still work at a basic level, in the workplace or local community. Where we have more in common doctrinally, we can pray and work together on specific tasks, such as evangelistic outreach or youth work. Prayer for the local community and mutual encouragement, I believe, are possible among Christians of widely different backgrounds. The very act of doing something together is constructive.

In our own circle of contacts, we have seen several examples. In one part of Zagreb, two denominations share the same building, meeting for services at different times. A Baptist church is also used separately by a Korean Presbyterian fellowship and an interdenominational Charismatic prayer group. In the UK, a whole building was donated by one denomination to another more rapidly growing fellowship, because the first group believed the latter could use the building more effectively. And in London, two churches—Baptist and Charismatic—have decided to merge and use one building to reach the community more effectively.

Unity in Relation to Numbers

It is vital, in our individualistic society, to understand that living and working together was the divine plan right from the beginning: "It is not good for the man to be alone" (Gen. 2:18). The old saying, "there is strength in numbers," is also true in the spiritual realm. We shall not make much of a dent in the enemy ranks by doing things in little independent groups.

A concerted, organized army is most effective, but large numbers are not essential when we work in unison with the Holy Spirit. Just look at the effect Gideon and his three hundred men had when they acted together, broke the jars, sounded their trumpets, lit their torches, and shouted, exactly as God told them (see Judg. 7:19-20).

Following God's plan, in complete step with one another and acting in reliance on God's strength, these three hundred apparently unremarkable men routed a Midianite and Amalekite army that covered the valley of Jezreel "thick as locusts" (Judg. 7:12). Seeing the battle was going their way, other Israelites joined in, and by the end of the day 120,000 enemy soldiers were dead. On a later occasion, when the Philistine army was "as numerous as the sand on the seashore" (1 Sam. 13:5), it only required two to agree. King Saul's son Jonathan gained the support of his bodyguard to climb a cliff and attack an enemy scouting group. The Philistines panicked, and the whole army was completely routed (see 1 Sam. 14). That is the sort of victory we can expect when we stand together in unity! (See First Samuel 14:6b.)

UNITY, NOT UNIFORMITY

Living and working in Central Europe, I have traveled to many places over the years. I visited the beautiful cathedral in Krakow in Poland, and walked around the spectacular old city of Prague, its castle dominating the skyline above the river Vltava. I have also gazed down on the spires of the Hungarian parliament building from the battlements of the royal castle of Buda in the center of Budapest. These places are wonderful structural testaments to the creative capabilities of past generations.

The Drabness of Uniformity

But I have also witnessed the heritage of forty-plus years of communist rule: the concrete office blocks dominating the center of Warsaw; the rusting remnants of factories in the provinces of the Czech Republic; and the grey, depressing apartment blocks ("people cages," as a Croatian friend calls them) that ring the picturesque city centers in Prague, Zagreb, and Halle. In the ex-German Democratic Republic, the style was referred to as *Plattenbau* (slab-building), shoddily put together from innumerable, prefabricated slabs of concrete and reinforced steel. The result was a dull environment in which individuality was suppressed and adherence to imposed uniformity demanded. I saw this monotony firsthand, during the 1970s and 1980s, when people queued for hours in front of empty shop windows in the hope of acquiring a few basic essentials.

When the "iron curtain" was torn down in the early 1990s, it was wonderful to see how color and variety returned to the shops and pedestrians' clothes. New stores opened up, and old buildings were restored to their previous beauty. Even the *Plattenbau* buildings received new coats of paint in yellow, pink, orange, and green.

The Immense Variety in Nature

The uniformity of socialism was dull, drab, and depressing. This is not what God has created or planned for His people. The world is a marvelous "box of chocolates" (as Forrest Gump described it), full of surprises and variety. It is not just the spectacular blaze of color that bursts out in spring. There are the diverse species and designs of birds and butterflies; the extraordinary number of different beetle species (around 300,000 worldwide!); the various colors and consistencies of the rocks and soil; and the unique diversity of colors, shapes, and expressions of the human face. God absolutely loves diversity! He has put more variety into His creation than we are even able to investigate or catalog.

Diversity in the Body of Christ

Now, if God has introduced such immense variety into the current universe, which is groaning under the influence of sin (see Rom. 8:20-22), how much more diversity is He already incorporating into the new eternal spiritual creation (see 2 Cor. 5:1-5)? *God through His Holy Spirit is building us together as a single, multi-functioning, God-glorifying, spiritual household, replete with unimaginable diversity.* True unity is not uniformity! It is the deliberate commitment of our diverse abilities, time, and energies to serve one another and jointly work to build God's Kingdom and give Him the glory.

Ephesus—at the mouth of the river Caystros on the west coast of what is now Turkey—had been a terminus for camel trains and a wealthy commercial gateway to the East under the Persians long before it was taken by the Greek Emperor, Alexander the Great, in 334 B.C. It became the capital of Asia Minor and a major port under the Romans two hundred years later. The site of the temple of the goddess Artemis (Diana to the Romans) since Persian times, it became a center for worship of the Roman Emperor. Its population then was thought to be around a quarter of a million. It was a melting pot of peoples, cultures, religions, and trades—full of merchants, travelers, soldiers, slaves, and citizens of varying status. And out of this diversity, the church in Ephesus was established.

To this church, Paul says, "Maintain the unity God has given you. Enjoy the variety God has provided, but do not force your opinions and doctrines on others. Accept diversity, and use it to encourage one another" (see Eph. 4; 5). He goes on to warn the Christians not to bring the city's immorality into the life of the church. Maintaining the unity of the Spirit involves recognizing our own inadequacies; because of our weaknesses, we need each other for support. We need to show practical concern for one another across the whole Church. This does not just mean preaching in different congregations or sharing joint evangelistic outreaches, but visiting the elderly, getting together in parents organizations in schools, sharing our cars for the journey to work, or supporting each other in complementary businesses. Putting our diverse abilities to work in such helpful, practical ways inevitably draws Christians together in spirit as well. Our unity and Christ-likeness is perhaps most clearly expressed in the unglamorous practical service we give each other—especially toward people who are not in "our own congregation."

CREATIVE HARMONY

Nehemiah was not the first to discover the value of using a variety of capable people to work on the project God had given him. Much earlier, when Solomon had started to build the temple to God's glory, he had scoured the Middle East for craftsmen with a variety of exceptional skills, as David his father had advised him (see 2 Chron. 2; 1 Chron. 28:21). And David certainly knew that working and living together brings blessing, as it was he who had written, "How good and pleasant it is when brothers live together in unity!" (Ps. 133:1).

Complementing Through Diversity

David had learned this from the distressed, indebted, discontented men who came to him at the cave of Adullam, when he first fled from King Saul (see 1 Sam. 22:2). They shared his life in exile and suffered with their leader when their wives, children, and possessions were taken by the marauding Amalekites (see 1 Sam. 30:1-6). They also shared his joy when they recaptured all that had been taken as well as the plunder the Amalekites had accumulated (see 1 Sam. 30:17-20). These men became the nucleus of David's army, sharing great victories, and several of them became known as David's mighty men (see 2 Sam. 23:8-39). Oh yes, David knew exactly how much he owed his men, who had lived with him in extremity, fought with him through great dangers, and celebrated his coronation and conquests. He knew by experience the blessing that comes through living together in unity, with one purpose, one heart, and one mind. It was the variety of strengths of his men, as well as their dedication to him and each other, that made David strong.

God has placed an immense variety of abilities within His Church, since "to each one of us grace has been given" (Eph. 4:7). Paul lists in Romans 12:6-8 some of these grace-gifts. They include prophesying, serving, teaching, encouraging, contributing to needs, leadership, and showing mercy. These are so wide-ranging that nobody is left without at least one grace to add to the mix. In another letter, Paul emphasizes that all gifts and types of service are provided by the same Lord, through the same Spirit, specifically for the "common good" (1 Cor. 12:4-7). Each of us, individually and as a group, can use our unique combination of gifts to benefit the whole Body. We cannot simply rely on the pastor or priest. The Church needs all kinds of people and giftings to "carry out the ministry"!

This does not just mean within the local church—even different ways of looking at the Bible and its practical application enrich

God's people. Nowadays, there is room for new gifts and abilities in art, dance, films, and computing. We should be encouraging one another to identify our gifts and use them so that everyone gains the benefit. There is the computer expert who can help remove a virus or the electrician willing to set up the conference sound system; the Christian lawyer who is able to advise on buying a property, or the teacher willing to give a young student extra tuition. How about setting up a Website with links to various Christian companies and individuals offering services? Creativity has no boundaries.

One women's group in Zagreb, consisting largely of foreign women married to Croatian men, has been a great blessing. These potentially lonely women not only encourage one another, but also draw their predominantly unbelieving husbands into the social group. Another group of mature Christian women established strong interdenominational contacts and initiated a variety of practical community activities. Each woman has used her own strengths— cooking, handicraft, teaching, music, children's work—to bless the others, irrespective of the local church they attend. The result is that differences can now be discussed without rancor, barriers are being broken down, and the vision to reach the city is growing.

From a practical point of view, it is worth considering the diversity among the disciples, contacts, and friends around Jesus. There were fishermen, a tax collector, a variety of women, mothers, an ex-prostitute, some high-ranking religious leaders, and even a thieving keeper of the treasury. Jesus maintained contacts with all of them. Perhaps the secret is that these contacts were at different levels. Peter, James, and John appear to have been closest to Him, though His mother, Mary, was frequently in His vicinity. The other nine disciples spent three years continuously traveling with Him, and Jesus often stayed at the house of Mary, Martha, and Lazarus. Others spent less time with Him, but the rich businessman, Joseph of Arimathea, was still sufficiently close to Jesus to be willing to donate an expensive tomb for His burial. In fact, Jesus' definition of friends and supporters was very broad. When the disciples complained that someone else was trying to exorcise demons in His name, Jesus' response was, "Whoever is not against us is for us" (Mark 9:40). Clearly, Jesus was ready to be associated with others well beyond His immediate entourage.

I believe we can also maintain the unity of the Spirit by fostering contacts with other Christians at different levels. With some, we may have much in common and enjoy a close relationship. With others, we share interests and occupations. Where our paths and activities intersect, it is best to develop relationships with those who love the Lord Jesus, irrespective of doctrine and creed, rather than to avoid them. Our broad diversity can demonstrate how God's love can unite us.

Diversity in Leadership

Leadership in the Church should also have diverse qualities (see Eph. 4:11). First, there are the apostles, who may be seen in our day and age as Holy Spirit-commissioned construction pioneers. Then there are the prophets, the IT department, providing the Church with topical Holy Spirit-inspired information, and the evangelists who represent the marketing agents, taking the Gospel out into the world. Finally, there are the pastors and teachers, who can be viewed as the spiritual health professionals, shepherding and exhorting the Church. None of these are "management" positions, as we might consider from a business point of view. In the concept Paul presents to the Ephesians, each of these tasks is needed to prepare and train others to be workers (not consumers) in God's Kingdom, to become knowledgeable and mature (not spoon-fed) believers, able to make their own independent contributions to the normal functioning of the Body (see Eph. 4:12-13).

Here, there is no suggestion of hierarchical superiority. The goal is to "reach unity in the faith" and to attain "to the whole measure of the fulness of Christ" (Eph. 4:13). And just in case we get the wrong idea about being like Christ, Paul writes to the Philippians that this involves becoming a servant to others, even being ready to die to help other Christians (see Phil. 2:7-8). Paul comes back to his recurrent theme, urging the believers once again, with all the conviction he can muster, to be "like-minded, having the same love, being one in spirit and purpose. Do nothing out of selfish ambition or vain conceit, but in humility consider others better than yourselves" (Phil. 2:2-4).

We need the variety of God's gifts—across denominational and confessional divides—to maintain our vertical orientation toward Him. Too often, because of our unbalanced attitudes to each other, the local church looks like the leaning tower of Pisa!

Among the leaders in the first church in Jerusalem were Peter, an uneducated, impetuous fisherman, an apostle and pastor from the backwoods of Galilee; Barnabas, a wealthy Cypriot, peacemaker, evangelist, and later apostle; and Stephen, a charismatic Greek deacon, healer, and evangelist. In the church in Antioch—where the followers of The Way first became known as Christians—the leaders included Barnabas; Simeon the Black, probably from Africa; Lucius from Cyrene, a port on the North African coast; and Manaen, a boyhood friend of King Herod, a decidedly questionable heritage! (See Acts 13:1.) In these early churches, race, culture, position, breeding, education, and religious background meant nothing. It was spiritual maturity, sensitivity to the Holy Spirit, and commitment to the Lord and one another that characterized these leaders (see Acts 13:2-3). What a challenge to our often middle-class, denominational, institutional, parochial attitudes! We do not have to think, act, speak, or even believe the same thing. As we considered earlier, Paul disagreed with Barnabas (see Acts 15:37-40); Peter (see Gal. 2:11); and possibly Apollos (see 1 Cor. 3:4-6). But it is clear that Paul did not want such differences to break the unity of faith that he shared with these men. Using all the diversity that God has given us, positively and creatively, the Church "grows and builds itself up in love, as each part does its work" (Eph. 4:16).

Harmonizing Together

We do not have to be growing at the same rate or using a similar method of evangelism or relationship development. God twice promises the nation of Israel that if they obey Him and try to live together in harmony, then peace "like a river" will accompany them (Isa. 48:18; 66:12). The picture is one of a large, wide river, gently flowing through beautiful, fertile countryside, providing a fruitful and refreshing environment.

The flow of liquids in all channels (e.g., riverbeds, hosepipes, or arteries) is always faster in the center than at the edges, where it is slowed by friction. In a wide, peaceful river, some of the water at the edge may even accumulate weeds and algae. But the peace and effective functioning of the ecosystem is the result of all its components—fast and slow moving. Equally, the peace of a united Church is the result of each part flowing in harmony with the others.

Elaine and I have enjoyed some wonderful concerts by the Zagreb Philharmonic Orchestra. Before a concert, some of the musicians are often still tuning up. Played independently, the instruments are discordant and irritating; then in comes the conductor, who calls the orchestra to order and lifts his baton. As he moves his arm, the musicians respond as one, and a mellow, harmonious wave of integrated sound fills the air!

By making a deliberate effort to combine our social, professional, community, and various outreach activities with other groups of Christians, rather than playing our own individual tunes, the harmony of a united Church will attract many more to join us.

Endnotes

1. http://thinkexist.com/quotation/control_your_own_destiny_or_someone_else_will/151582.html.

2. Mark Stibbe and Andrew Williams, *Breakout* (Milton Keynes, UK: Authentic Media, 2008), 139.

CHAPTER 5

THE ADHESIVE POWER OF LOVE

IN ESSENTIALS UNITY, IN NON-ESSENTIALS LIBERTY,
IN ALL THINGS LOVE.

—St. Augustine, A.D. 354–430

My mother disliked having to clean my bedroom when I was a boy. All open spaces were filled with model ships, while planes hung on threads from the ceiling. My brother's creations occupied the space I had not claimed! We spent many hours constructing those models. With our first attempts, we glued the pieces together quickly, to see what the finished article looked like. This made painting awkward, as some inside pieces could not be reached. Subsequently, we took time to clean and paint the pieces before putting them together. The finished article looked much more realistic. The closer we followed the instructions, the better the model looked.

God likes joining things together as well! In fact, He is the master builder. Paul tells us that we are being "joined together" in Christ Jesus (Eph. 2:21-22). Like the models my brother and I made, the best results come when each individual piece is cleaned and prepared. When everything is glued together, we see the finished product, not the individual parts. Small pieces only become noticeable if one of them is broken or missing.

God also wants the final article to look good and function perfectly. If the builders do not keep to the master plan, then, like our early, hurried models, the final result looks unfinished. The crucial technique in building plastic models is to apply the glue carefully and precisely. Too much in the wrong place and the glue overflows and spoils the plastic. Too little and one of the pieces can fall off later. Done properly, the adhesive holds the pieces together and is not visible in the final model. The same applies to Christian relationships.

Joined in Partnership

Marriage between a man and woman is described scripturally as being united, becoming "one flesh" (Gen 2:24). The two are "glued together" physically and emotionally. Totally committed to one another, they become a single functioning union. In contrast, promiscuous, casual sex is like being stuck to several different partners in an amorphous lump. In this case, separation leaves physical, emotional, and spiritual wounds. By analogy, God is in the process of gluing individuals "from every tribe and language and people and nation" precisely together as one Body, the Church (Rev. 5:9).

Paul emphasizes that the Church is made up of different parts, each member using the gifts given by the Holy Spirit "for the common good" (1 Cor. 12:7). But all these gifts and abilities, by themselves, have no spiritual value, says Paul, if we do not have love:

> *If I speak in the tongues of men and of angels, but have not love, I am only a resounding gong or a clanging cymbal. If I have the gift of prophecy and can fathom all mysteries and all knowledge, and if I have a faith that can move mountains, but have not love, I am nothing. If I give all I possess to the poor and surrender my body to the flames, but have not love, I gain nothing (1 Corinthians 13:1-3).*

Jesus Himself said, "If you love Me, you will obey what I command" (John 14:15). And in the same discourse He explains what this command is: "A new command I give you: love one another. As I have loved you, so you must love one another" (John 13:34). Love for other Christians is not an option! It is not something we decide to do on the basis of whether we get on with them, like them, or share the same theology. Loving one another is God's command! As in the marriage relationship, love is the glue which—when applied in the right amount in exactly the right place—holds everything together!

Aligning Words With Actions

When we refer to the Church as one, we tend to think of our own local church. Broader unity in the love of Christ may be tacitly assumed, but rarely consciously sought. Yet, according to Jesus, this should be a natural response to His love for us. As we saw earlier, love for each other should characterize our outward appearance as the Church.

After His resurrection, Jesus asked Peter three times whether he loved Him (see John 21:15-17). Jesus wanted a heartfelt response and kept questioning Peter to be sure that the answer was real. When we start to understand and respond to the amazing, unlimited dimensions of Jesus' love for us (see Eph. 3:18-19), then the overriding importance of being at peace and unity with other believers begins to dawn. Love has to be the basis for all our relationships in the Spirit. If only our lips and intellect are involved, it is not going to last.

This appears to have been the case in the church in Corinth. It was relatively large, with businessmen, educated intellectuals, and a wealth of spiritual gifts. But they had not learned how to use these gifts. Members tended to employ the gifts for themselves rather than for others. Paul explains that love, the glue that binds the different gifts and abilities together, was missing. So let us see how love works.

WHAT LOVE IS NOT

In one of the most beautiful, inspired passages in Scripture, Paul distinguishes love from unloving behavior and explains how love can be recognized—by what it does and does not do:

Love is patient, love is kind. It does not envy, it does not boast, it is not proud. It is not rude, it is not self-seeking, it is not easily angered, it keeps no record of wrongs. Love does not delight in evil but rejoices with the truth (1 Corinthians 13:4-6).

Love Is Not Proud

The opposite of love, Paul explains, is not hate. It is pride, selfishness, and envy. Ultimately, pride is the most basic of all sins. It is what led lucifer, the "son of the dawn" and his followers to revolt against God and be driven out of Heaven (Isa. 14:12-15). It is the virus with which he infects every human being, and it is the essence of everything that raises itself against God because only God is good (see Matt. 19:17). By His very nature, "God is love" (1 John 4:16). Pride indicates a lack of love. In Corinth, the Christians had become infected with the attitudes of the bustling commercial city around them. They were proud of their wealth, intellect, and personal gifts; they were so concerned about guarding their own status that despite all the gifts in the church, the Body was coming "unstuck."

The cells and organs of the human body are all held together by sugary molecular glue—the adhesion molecules. These sticky molecules also pass on signals to cells to instruct them on how they should function. Genetic deficiency or pathological alteration of any type of adhesion molecule results in disease, impaired defense, increased infection, deficient wound healing, cancer, and so on.

By analogy, love, like adhesion molecules, not only holds the Body of Christ together but should also determine how we react toward each other and to unbelievers "outside" the Body. If the messages we pass on to one another are motivated by love, then the Body can grow and function in a healthy manner. This is why we are encouraged to spend time together with other Christians as often as possible (see Heb. 10:24-25). Conversely, if we start sending incorrect signals, if we are not interacting with one another in the right spirit, or if the glue of love is missing, then things start to go very wrong. Allowing love to be ousted by envy led Cain to kill his brother Abel (see Gen. 4:5,8) and Prince Absalom to rebel against his father King David (see 2 Sam. 15). When her love (see 1 Sam. 18:20) changed to derision, Michal's marriage to King David soured, and she became infertile (see 2 Sam. 6:16-23). The apostle Paul tells us that many physical (and presumably psychological) problems, even deaths, in a church can result when we come together as a divided fellowship and fail to recognize our mutual participation in the Body of Christ (see 1 Cor. 11:18-20,29-30).

Love Is Not Self-Seeking

It is not a natural human response to abstain from boasting or self-seeking. The pride that robs us of our love for one another comes in a wide variety of disguises. These may be very thinly concealed when someone is really pleased with his or her gifts. This type of pride often peeks through upfront abilities, like singing, dancing, or playing an instrument. We have all met such performers who take every opportunity to laud their own gift. Church leaders are particularly open to pride because of their public exposure. Yet there are also wonderfully gifted Christians with great humility.

One of our good friends is a pastor and evangelist in the UK. Despite the fact that he is much sought after as a preacher and teacher, his whole demeanor is one of love and care. You have the feeling when talking to him that you are the most important person he has spoken to that week. Even his wife says he is like a saint at home! Such people cement relationships.

Love Is Not Easily Angered

There are also more subtle ways for pride to creep into our relationships. Often we take offense at other Christians. Perhaps something they said or did hurt us—or they hold a different set of beliefs—so we refuse to have anything more to do with them. This is not avoiding compromise; it is sin and a lack of love—plain and simple!

In his book *Love Covers,* Paul E. Billheimer provides an eloquent appeal to the Church to allow love, not doctrinal purity, to determine our relationships with other believers:

> Since disunity in the Body probably sends more people to hell than open sin, breaking fellowship over differences in those standards or practices which are not actually necessary to salvation is a greater sin than the supposed error which precipitated the breach.[1]

Having discussed some of these practices, Billheimer writes, "We shall never be united by conceptual truth, church policy, liturgy, or any canon or confession of faith—only by agape love."[2] He challenges us to seek deliverance from the "idolatry of personal opinion" and recognize that:

> when one refuses to fellowship with another who is organically united to the Body of Christ because he differs on nonessential matters, he is not only creating schism in the Body, but bringing grief to the heart of Christ. He has been "conned" by the one who masquerades as an angel of light.[3]

Without love to guide us, we become oversensitive to our own sense of importance. This makes us easy to upset, irritate, and annoy. Paul says that love is not easily angered; it does not hold grudges or delight in getting its own back (see 1 Cor. 13:5-6). We need God's help and strength.

Love Keeps No Record of Wrong

When hurts are not forgiven and healed by love for one another, bitterness usually creeps in, because we "keep records of wrong" (see 1 Cor. 13:5). This is something we are all prone to do. We store away the instances when someone has said or done something that has been hurtful. Then, at an opportune moment, we open up the filing cabinet again and gossip about all the unpleasant details of the event. As a result, we imprint the experience indelibly on our memory and enhance the hurt.

In contrast to the kindness and forgiveness generated by love, bitterness causes division and illness. We are exhorted by the writer to the Hebrews to "see to it that no-one misses the grace of God and that no bitter root grows up to cause trouble and defile many" (Heb. 12:15). And at the end of his chapter on unity, Paul exhorts the Ephesians to:

> *Get rid of all bitterness, rage and anger, brawling and slander, along with every form of malice. Be kind and compassionate to one another, forgiving each other, just as in Christ God forgave you* (Ephesians 4:31-32).

Lack of love and forgiveness not only damages the Body of Christ, it also injures the unloving person. There is plenty of evidence to indicate that the mental stress resulting from bitterness and unforgiveness is highly detrimental to health.[4] Jesus clearly describes the self-destructive effects of unforgiveness in His parable of the unmerciful servant (see Matt. 18:21-35). The servant could not repay a huge debt which his master mercifully cancelled, releasing the servant from his obligation. The ungrateful servant then refused to forgive his fellow servant the small debt he owed him and had his colleague put in prison. In response, the master overturned his cancellation of the debt and handed over the ungrateful servant "to be tortured" *until he repaid his debt* (see Matt. 18:34).

Jesus says that we shall receive the same treatment if we do not forgive our brothers (see Matt. 18:35). Our lack of forgiveness toward our fellow believer brings back on our own heads the guilt that God is unable to remove and "tortures" our state of mind! How much anguish of heart and soul we could spare ourselves if we forgave and sought reconciliation with believers from whom we have separated ourselves in anger. This is something we shall explore further in Chapter 7.

Love Does Not Envy

The same self-destructive principle applies to envy. Proverbs 14:30 tells us that "a heart at peace gives life to the body, but envy rots the bones." It is like osteoporosis, destroying the internal structure of the Church and facilitating its collapse.

The society we live in is full of envy—envy of wealth, of celebrities and success; envy of athletes and of our neighbors. It is a widespread cancer in the business world: envy of a colleague's promotion, of that big deal or that handsome bonus our good-for-nothing rival received. But this tumor has spread into Christian circles as well. Are we envious of the new building another church community has built—or of the voice of the singer in the worship group? Do we listen to the deacon's prayer and wish we could be as eloquent? Love "does not envy" (1 Cor. 13:4). I tell you, if we learned to love each other with the care and self-sacrifice that Jesus showed, we would not even think of being envious. Our love for the Lord would make us all much more attractive toward one another!

It was not only in their quarreling that Paul accused the Corinthians of being like little children. He also confronted their need always to have their own way (see 1 Cor. 3:3). "That's mine!" "I want what he's got!" "It's not fair!" Paul subsequently says, "Grow up, put childish ways behind you, and make love your aim" (see 1 Cor. 13:11). We should be ready to relinquish our need to be "in the right." My rights were crucified with Christ, and now He is living His life in me (see Gal. 2:20). The Spirit of Jesus Christ in you and me is much more concerned about putting us back to rights than proving that we are right.

WHAT LOVE DOES

It is God's love that transforms us into a beautiful Body. We know from scientific studies that physical attractiveness—across a wide variety of different ethnic backgrounds—is related to specific proportions of the face and body. These usually reflect health, fitness, youth, and reproductive capability.

Love Makes Us Look Beautiful

This is equally true of the Body of Christ—the way we are put together determines our beauty in the eyes of others. As Jesus said, "By this all men will know that you are My disciples, if you love one another" (John 13:35). If we are born (again) by the Spirit of God, then His hereditary beauty should be visible in each of us.

We are not recognized as spiritually beautiful Christians because we know our Bibles, preach the Gospel to everyone who crosses our path, demonstrate against abortion, go regularly to church services, or adhere rigidly to the traditions of our denomination. Our beauty is determined entirely by the dimensions of our love for Jesus and for one another! And that means our love for *all* other believers in Christ. God's love is demonstrated by what it does in and through us for the benefit of everyone with whom we come into contact, but it is shown especially by what we do for those who are members of God's family (see Gal. 6:10). In fact, John says that if someone is not able to show love toward another member of God's family, then it is questionable whether they really love God at all (see 1 John 4:19-21).

Love Is Patient, Love Is Kind

Jesus, as our example, was patient with His disciples when they pestered Him with exasperating questions or were slow to grasp what He was saying (see Luke 8:25; 24:25). He showed great forbearance with the crowds who kept looking for Him, even when He wanted time alone and needed a break (see Luke 9:10-11). He did not ignore persistent beggars, but was kind and considerate toward them, and unlike His disciples, He was perfectly willing to allow children to disturb Him (see Luke 18:35-43; Matt. 19:13-14). Jesus—who more than 100 times in the Gospels is reported as saying, "I tell you the truth"—publicly exposed deceit in those who were deliberately trying to trick Him (see Matt 22:15-22). But He was gentle and supportive toward the hemorrhaging woman who was afraid of telling Him the truth (see Mark 5:32-34). His protective love repeatedly reached out to all the inhabitants of Jerusalem despite the fact that they were about to reject and kill Him (see Matt. 23:37). And in His dying moments, He was concerned that His mother should be taken care of by John (see John 19:27).

He put complete trust in Peter's leadership qualities even though the disciple had let Him down terribly (see John 18:25-27; 21:15-17). He gave hope to John the Baptist when he was going through despair in prison (see Matt. 11:2-5). And He persevered in His ministry, never giving up on His goal to die for you and me, even though He underwent intense mental and spiritual agony and separation from His Father (see Phil. 2:8; Luke 22:42-44; Matt. 27:46). Never having failed in His love for us, He is now able to save completely anyone who comes to Him in faith (see Heb. 7:24-25). This is the example of practical love we should be following, rather than justifying ourselves or comparing ourselves favorably with other Christians. Let us seek to be of one mind and spirit with Jesus, sharing His love with one another (see Phil. 2:5). This is the practical love that radiates Christ's beauty to everyone around us.

As a teenager, I was not very likeable. I tended to compensate for my small stature by bragging. Brought up in a strict, conservative Christian home, I did not drink alcohol or go to the cinema. I was therefore considered something of a weirdo. When I left for university, I dutifully went to church on Sundays, but during the week tried to catch up on everything I had "missed out" on at home. Most members of the students' Christian Union were wary of this loud, opinionated little guy who ignored standards of good Christian behavior.

At a church youth club, I met a young man who was very different. Phil Price was very enthusiastic about Jesus, but still went to parties and discos and enjoyed playing sports. He seemed to get on with everyone and was invariably positive in his attitudes. I cannot remember Phil ever making any negative comment about what I did. He just accepted me as I was and encouraged me, by his example, to get to know Jesus better. Quite different from many Christians I had known before, he had a genuine love for the Lord that was infectious. I went with him to charismatic services, and as a result, I was filled with the Holy Spirit, giving my life new direction and strength. When I left London, I lost contact with Phil, who later was tragically killed in a plane crash. But I am so grateful to the Lord for introducing me to such a naturally loving Christian!

Love Protects and Supports

We all need these loving Christian relationships for encouragement and support. Human organs only function properly when each cell is stuck to those around it and regularly supplied with oxygen and nutrients from the blood. It would not do for one group of cells to detach themselves from the others. Not only would they die from lack of support and nutrition, but there would be localized injury to the organ as well. It is by:

> *speaking the truth **in love**...*[that] *we will in all things grow up into Him who is the Head, that is, Christ. From Him the whole body, joined and held together by every supporting ligament, grows and builds itself up **in love**, as each part does its work* (Ephesians 4:15-16).

The reason we have ligaments to hold our joints together is to maintain flexibility. A joint, like the elbow or knee, is a complex organization of protective cartilage, lubricating joint fluid, tendons, and ligaments to hold the muscle in place and ensure effective movement. Injury or arthritis damages the joint and impairs mobility. Likewise, in some parts of the Church, through religiosity and lack of love, flexibility toward other believers is lost, and local irritation arises, causing damage to relationships and cooperation.

We should be considerate and supportive, but also respectful, "speaking the truth in love." As Paul says, our conversation should be "always full of grace, seasoned with salt" (Col. 4:6). This means we may have to bite our tongues at times, when tempted to be unnecessarily critical or argumentative, giving the benefit of the doubt rather than pushing our own opinion. This is particularly true when talking about Christians of different persuasions. It means consciously taking control of critical thoughts before they turn into words. It is not constructive to make disparaging comments, for instance, about the style of a fellow believer's prayer. But challenging a brother whose actions are damaging his own spiritual welfare can be a true service of love.

Have you noticed how negative gossip about a person colors our subsequent thoughts and attitudes to them? We start to believe what was said and begin to lose trust, just because of a negative comment. Trust is a fragile treasure that too easily can be shattered. *I believe it is our spoken words that maintain or disrupt unity.* It is no coincidence that Brother Roger—the Lutheran clergyman who founded the Ecumenical Community of Taizé in France (a retreat center for reconciliation), and who was respected globally by Christians and leaders of all shades and colors—avoided, all his life, harsh words about others.[5] As my mother used to remind me, "If you cannot say anything positive, then it is better not to say anything at all."

Love Rejoices With the Truth, but Makes Allowances

Honesty in our dealings with each other and the Lord is very important. This is the way trust is built, a fact that became existentially clear to Ananias and Sapphira (see Acts 5:1-11). Moreover, we are exhorted to be clear in our own minds where we stand with regard to acceptable behavior (see Rom. 14:14,16). But in the same passage, Paul warns that we should not allow our zeal for "Christian correctness" in the external observance of our faith to unlovingly run roughshod over a fellow believer's different religious sensitivities (see Rom. 14:15). Jesus, Himself, is the Truth (see John 14:6) and was always able to uncover layers of denial or concealment in the people He confronted. But He did this graciously, without forcing the point. If we too are gracious with our opinions and attitudes, we shall be able to draw closer, creating the opportunity to "speak the truth in love." We do not have to emphasize our differences when sharing in prayer or practical work in the community. Jesus regularly overrode human interpretations of the law—whether about eating on the Sabbath (see Matt. 12:1-8); stoning an adulteress (see John 8:3-11); or (as a Jewish man) helping a promiscuous Samaritan woman (see John 4:7-29)—in order to show grace and practical love toward others. How important is formally correct religious practice when spiritual unity is at stake? Not very important at all! If we pray differently, preach differently, or praise differently, does that have to come between us as integral members of Christ's Body? I am convinced it should not.

Love Encourages Spiritual Gifts

The good health of the whole Church is dependent on each of us encouraging the other to grow, develop our abilities, and reach out for the gifts of the Holy Spirit (see 1 Cor. 14:1). While love is the glue that holds us together, the work of the Holy Spirit in our lives, individually and corporately, is the lifeblood of the Body of Christ. If we are following the "way of love," then we should be instinctively desiring the fullness and gifts of the Holy Spirit which He gives "for the common good" and "as He determines" (1 Cor. 14:1; 12:7,11). In fact, the way of love and spiritual gifts are inseparable.

Human love has a tendency to be soft and distracting, as anyone knows who watches a young couple! Then again, focused, task-orientated people can be inconsiderate in their attitudes toward others. The Holy Spirit, through His gifts and fruit, enables us to achieve the balance between love and purpose. The diversified and actively growing Body of Christ cannot do without the gifts and power of the Holy Spirit to sustain, empower, and transform us into the likeness of Jesus. Sadly, though, we often allow our prejudices to impede His work.

When some of the manifestations of the Holy Spirit do not suit neighboring churches, pride and unloving attitudes appear on both sides! One overemphasizes the gifts of the Spirit, which may be rejected by the other. So instead of unity through the bond of love, isolation and division break down the integrity of the local Body of Christ. This is not a beautiful sight and is likely to repel rather than attract unbelievers. But if members of the churches have been in regular contact in mundane ways—meeting for coffee, playing sports, helping neighbors—mutual love and respect will tend to encourage joint celebration of the Holy Spirit's work.

Love Covers

We should be actively seeking to help others, whoever they are, whatever their background: caring for the weak, providing for the poor, welcoming the stranger, training and encouraging all those who are hungry for more of God. Peter says, *"Above all,* love each other deeply, because love covers over a multitude of sins" (1 Pet. 4:8).

Nothing is more important for the believing Christian than to show practical and gracious love to others who know and love the Lord. Even large theological differences can be bridged in practical love between Christians whose faith rests on a shared life in the Spirit, received by personal acceptance of redemption through Jesus Christ: "For in Christ Jesus…the *only* thing that counts is faith expressing itself through love" (Gal. 5:6). When we lovingly help to restore a fellow believer who has slipped back into a sinful lifestyle, we "cover over a multitude of sins" (James 5:19-20).

Demonstrated, practical love between us is more important than gifts or ministries and is the most effective way to reveal the transforming power of the resurrected Savior to those who have never had the privilege and joy to know Him: "Therefore, as we have opportunity, let us do good to all people, especially to those who belong to the family of believers" (Gal. 6:10).

Love Drives out Fear

There is one other outcome of the love of God that Paul does not specifically address in First Corinthians 13; that is, "perfect love drives out fear" (1 John 4:18). Fear arises because we sense that we have something to lose. It thrives on uncertainty and lack of knowledge, and its presence indicates that we have not yet learned to love perfectly.

We all tend to slip back into self-reliance, self-preservation, and self-glorification. But each time we do so, we open ourselves up once again to fear: fear of letting someone down, fear of failure, fear of making a fool of ourselves, fear of harm or danger, fear for our family, fear of being influenced by wrong doctrine, fear of letting God down by working with Christians of another denomination, fear that we will be branded as heretics. These fears are based on our lack of understanding and faith in the greatness and goodness of our Father who never lets us down. We have to learn over and over and over again that "God is our refuge and strength, an ever-present help in trouble. Therefore we will not fear" (Ps. 46:1-2). His love "always protects, always trusts, always hopes, always perseveres" (1 Cor. 13:7). It is unconditional, unstinting, unlimited, and freely available in and for every situation. His "love never fails" (1 Cor. 13:8) and can always be drawn upon, especially in our dealings with our fellow believers.

It is often said that love is blind. When someone is head-over-heels in love, he or she can no longer see the faults, only the beauty of the adored partner. This rather confused state can be inconvenient in everyday life. But to so love the Lord that we lose sight of the potential risks of following Him gives us new strength and purpose. Our fear that something could go wrong must be transformed into confident expectation that God is always working together with us for good (see Rom. 8:24). Living a life of love means deliberately handing over our lives and plans every day as an offering to the Lord (see Rom. 12:1; Eph. 5:2). In practice, this means deliberating looking for opportunities to spur other believers on "towards love and good deeds" (Heb. 10:24).

JOINED TOGETHER

With some of the model planes my brother and I made, the wings and fuselage had to be put together separately and then later glued to make the whole plane. This is how Airbus Industrie builds its jet aircraft, making separate parts in different countries and then flying them to Toulouse to be attached in the final steps of construction. These different sections could be compared to Christian churches and groups around the world. Many are carefully guarding their small piece of the Body but have overlooked the fact that we all need to be attached so that the Body can be complete.

Start Small

How do we live together in unity? How do we encourage one another to show greater love in charitable actions toward one another (see Heb. 10:24)? Starting from our common commitment to follow Jesus, it is the small decisions we make that maintain our unity. It is the decision to have coffee regularly with my Baptist neighbor; to travel in the same train compartment with the deacon from the Pentecostal church; and to spend ten minutes each morning praying with my Roman Catholic colleague for God's blessing on our workplace. Such apparently insignificant things, both positive and negative, can lead very rapidly to visible effects (see Matt. 17:20; James 1:14-15). If we make those small decisions, based on love and mutual respect for one another, our unity will be sustained when the crunch of a major challenge comes. Small decisions made wrongly, though, mount up to a wall of division when we face an important issue.

John tells us that love is being ready to give to our brothers, particularly when one of them is in need (see 1 John 3:16-17). This can include small things, but there is no upper limit. We can start in our own fellowship, but also assist other believers we know. Recently, we were able to help the leader of a small church who was short of money. When God sees we can be trusted in small things, He can also trust us with the bigger tasks (see Luke 16:10).

Building Bridges

Probably the best place to show practical unity is where theological opinions are least important—in the workplace. We shall consider this in the last chapter. Praying with and for Christian colleagues is a very effective way to show love for one another.

We need to set goals that transcend religious practice or theological differences, based on our unity in the Spirit. The desire of our hearts, that "by all possible means [we] might win some," then gives us a common purpose (1 Cor. 9:22). This goal might be to reach the homeless in the city, to establish a training center for ethical business management, or to improve the chances for youth in the city. Even wider, we can seek to reform the political life of the country or work for a spiritual and moral transformation of the society. Independently of our particular religious practice, such goals provide opportunities to combine and focus our diversity to tackle the issues.

Taizé community had a small beginning after the Second World War when Brother Roger and his sister started to care for children in need. By caring for persecuted Jews and captured German prisoners alike, the community showed God's love for all. The community is now recognized around the world by leaders of every type of church. As Brother Roger has said, love is the basis.

ENDNOTES

1. Paul E. Billheimer, *Love Covers*, 42.

2. Billheimer, *Love Covers*, 106.

3. Billheimer, *Love Covers*, 116.

4. E.L. Worthington, et al., "Forgiveness, Health, and Well-Being: A Review of Evidence for Emotional Versus Decisional Forgiveness, Dispositional Forgivingness, and Reduced Unforgiveness," *Journal of Behavioral Medicine* 30

(2007), 291-302; http://www.springerlink.com/content/
u6h40775322v6366/.

5. Brother Alois, "Homage to Brother Roger"; http://www.
    taize.fr/en_article6736.html.

CHAPTER 6

LIFTING THE VEIL

—Ralph Waldo Emerson, American poet,
lecturer, and essayist, 1803–1882

It is reported that when asked how he could turn a lump of white marble into a beautiful sculpture, Michelangelo said, "I saw the figure in the marble and chipped away until I set it free." Ludwig van Beethoven possessed similar genius and composed some of his greatest works, such as his Ninth "Choral" Symphony when he was completely deaf. He could "hear" the music in his mind. They both had a clear conception of what they wanted to create.

Jesus too had a vision of "the joy set before Him" (Heb. 12:2) which "was to create in Himself" a new Body, "a radiant church, without stain or wrinkle" (Eph. 2:15; 5:27). It was this vision which gave Him the strength to suffer crucifixion and death. The Son of God has had this image on His mind for all eternity, and it will be realized when the heavenly Bridegroom returns for His Bride. John tells us that although it is unclear to us what we shall look like, "we know that when He appears, we shall be like Him, for we shall see Him as He is" (1 John 3:2).

John knew what he was talking about. He had a glimpse of the extraordinary wonder of the Son of God in His divine glory when Jesus was transfigured (see Luke 9:28-36). The memory of the experience clearly remained indelibly impressed on his mind and heart because, much later, John testified that "we have seen His glory…full of grace and truth," avowing that each believer has received something of this grace (John 1:14,16). Now, the Holy Spirit is putting these pieces of the "grace jigsaw" back together again to reveal the glory of Christ in His Church.

I believe the greatest obstacle to unity in the Church is our inability or unwillingness to see that the glory of the Risen Lord is only revealed by the whole jigsaw picture of the Global Church. We concentrate just on our own few pieces, which give a disjointed and confusing picture of the beauty of Christ Jesus. Like Michelangelo, we need to see beyond the part of the rock at which we are chipping and keep in our mind's eye a vision of the whole finished work.

But how do we do this? How do we train ourselves to see beyond the immediate situation and live with a wider, higher vision? The answer I believe is found in Paul's words to the Corinthians (see 2 Cor. 3:7-18). He reminds them that Moses covered his head with a veil after speaking to God on Mount Sinai to avoid dazzling the Israelites with the glory of God reflected in their leader's face. Paul then says that the religious Jews of the day were still unable to see God's glory because of the veil of legalism with which they were covered. The veil could only be taken away by Christ; by believing in Him, "we, who with unveiled faces all reflect the Lord's glory, are being transformed into His likeness with ever-increasing glory, which comes from the Lord, who is the Spirit" (2 Cor. 3:18). The passage also suggests the picture of a bride, dressed and prepared for her wedding, whose veil is lifted to show her beauty, bathed in the reflected love of the groom.

There appear to be two principles at work here. One is that we need to be looking at Jesus, sharing His vision of the perfected

Church, currently undergoing transformation by the Holy Spirit (see Heb. 12:2). As we spend time with the Lord, read about Him, and get to know Him better, we should be constantly reminding ourselves that we are not just building individual, personal relationships between us and our Savior. As we learn more about the Head, we need to allow the Holy Spirit to reveal more about the rest of the Body and how we can function together to reveal the beauty and glory of Christ.

The other principle is that we need to keep the veil of religiosity, legalism, and separation out of our faces. Most of us do not even realize that the veil is still in place! We have adjusted completely to the traditional attitude that we should concentrate on building our local church and, by implication, the welfare of our particular denomination. We have not even realized that there is nothing in Scripture to tell us to do this! Whenever reference is made in the New Testament to the Kingdom of God or Heaven, the Church or the Body, it is frequently accompanied by an injunction directed toward us *all* to care for one another, churches in other countries included.

We pursue our own individual timetables, local evangelistic campaigns, and denominational organizations with remarkably scant regard for any other Christians. The growth occurring in our local churches we see as confirmation of the correctness of the separate furrow we are ploughing. Yet in standard business management teaching, the executive who appears to be successful in his own activities, but who is not following the corporate strategy is the first to be fired! It is crucially important to recognize the constituent parts of the veil we have drawn over our faces. The growth and ultimate glory of the Church depends on the removal of these obstacles. So what makes up this veil? What do we need to cut away to reveal the beauty of Christ Jesus to the world?

DISINTEREST AND PAROCHIALISM

When we first moved to Germany, it took us four to five weeks to find a church where we felt at home. The search was compounded by our lack of knowledge of German and the fact that most Protestant churches referred to themselves as "free evangelical churches"—a hangover from World War II when all denominations were forcibly combined. These included *Evangelisch-Freikichliche Gemeinden, Freie evangelische Gemeinden, Christlich Freikirchliche Gemeinden, Freie Christliche Gemeinden,* or simply *Christliche Gemeinden,* making distinction extremely difficult! To complicate things further, one church was on a weekend trip when we turned up on a Sunday morning!

The church we settled on was welcoming, and we started making a few (English-speaking) friends, particularly among other young families. Some older members, though, seemed strangely distant. We assumed this was language-related. After a couple of months, however, one of the middle-aged church members came up to me after the Sunday morning service and asked, "Is it true you have a doctor title?" Not knowing what he was getting at, I informed him that I did, and he visibly relaxed. It turned out that being a young family we were not quite in the "right" category. As soon as my title was known, I qualified for inclusion in the professional clique! Needless to say, we were not keen to be inducted into this exclusive group, choosing to maintain well-distributed contacts throughout the church.

It is all too easy to become parochial. Obviously, there are some people with whom we have a particularly good rapport, who tend to become our good friends. But we need to look beyond the end of our noses! It is a biological principle that inbreeding increases considerably the chances of genetic diseases and deformities arising in the offspring. The gene pool, diversity, and immune-defense reactions diminish considerably. The same is true in the spiritual realm. By becoming too inward-looking in our personal and corporate lives as Christians, we markedly enhance the chance of becoming spiritually impoverished. We are open to increasing attack by the enemy and the risk of developing "deformed" rather than "reformed" opinions and beliefs. Our spiritual children become equally deficient and unable to grow properly. *We need the stimulus of challenge by others who see things differently.* We should not be fearful of entering into discourse with a believer from another stream of tradition; on the contrary, with an open heart and mind, we can only benefit.

The Holy Spirit, the creative breath of God, is always on the move, doing something new. We should be aware of the direction He is taking within His Church. If we are too concerned about our own immediate interests, we are likely to overlook what God is doing and get left behind! We might even miss out on an encounter with an angel! (See Hebrews 13:2.)

LACK OF VISION AND COMFORT

In many churches, a lack of interest in contact with other believers is often due to the absence of vision in the home church. There is an old English proverb that says "a rolling stone gathers no moss." This could be paraphrased, "an active organism gathers no dust." A church that is pursuing a clear vision to impact the community will inevitably create opportunities to work together with other Christians. The need for mutual prayer, support, advice, and contact should be self-evident, though it is often completely overlooked. By "going it alone," we call on just a fraction of the resources available to the Church of God. Churches going nowhere start gathering dust and looking inward. They become rusty and slow, with little expectation that anything will change. Ultimately, without vision, a church fellowship begins to break up (see Prov. 29:18).

A clear vision is like a bugle call on the battlefield, rallying the troops to the commanding officer. When we know where we are going and why, this becomes an incentive to others to follow. Passion is infectious! Do you know where the Church is going?

An allied concern is ease and comfort. We have jobs, homes, cars, an average of 1.7 children, go to church on a Sunday morning, attend the Wednesday night home group when it fits in our schedule, and put some cash into the collection for the missionaries—when we remember. We do not think much about the little old lady struggling to get by on her pension, but that is the pastor's responsibility anyway. We have conversations with other Christians when we meet for the annual denominational conference, but they have their own circle of friends and prayer partners. Such churches Keith Green described in his song "Asleep in the Light":

> The world is sleeping in the dark
> That the church just can't fight
> 'Cause it's asleep in the light
> How can you be so dead
> When you've been so well fed
> Jesus rose from the grave
> And you, you can't even get out of bed.[1]

This was the state of the church in Laodicea, which God challenged to "be earnest, and repent" (Rev. 3:19). We tend to get our priorities completely wrong. Sure, we should all try to work for our living. But in our consumer society, it is important to stop now and then and consider what we *really* need. We do not have to be overly concerned even about the basic necessities for life. The Lord knows what we need, and He wants to provide for us if we will get our priorities right (see Matt. 6:33). When we put Jesus and our united extension of His Kingdom first, our physical needs will be met as a side benefit!

INSENSITIVITY TO AND DISINTEREST IN THE HOLY SPIRIT

When we are feeling comfortable, it is so easy to get out of the habit of either talking or listening to God. As with a radio, the less we tune out the interfering voices crowding the airwaves, the less distinct will be the voice to which we should be listening. Our short-term memory fills up with the thoughts and impressions that regularly enter our minds. If we are not hearing what God whispers to us by His Holy Spirit, it is hardly surprising that we do not even notice when connections to other Christians have been lost.

Is it any wonder then that we see little evidence of the work of the Holy Spirit in our churches? Should we be surprised that attendance is dwindling, church members are discontented, and no one is responding to the sermons that are being preached? The embers are glowing, and the members are going! The nineteenth-century evangelist and teacher, Andrew Murray, wrote 100 years ago, "Decay of membership in the church is due to a decay of membership in Christ."[2] Romans 8:14 says, "Those who are led by the Spirit of God are sons of God." So if we are not being led by the Spirit, our membership in God's family becomes less obvious. The unity of the Church is sustained by members acting in response to the voice of the Holy Spirit in their hearts.

Jim Cymbala tells how, as a young pastor, he took over the Brooklyn Tabernacle in the center of New York City, a crumbling church with 20 members and no money. God called him to pray and believe for a revival, and he saw the church grow to 6,000 members. He writes, "In too many churches today...there is little dependence on God's power to make an ongoing difference."[3] He continues,

> If we do not yearn and pray and expect God to stretch out his hand and do the supernatural, it will not happen...If we go on, week after week, filling the time with religious lectures and nothing more, God has little opportunity to move.[4]

We must listen to and believe what God is saying by His Holy Spirit and *expect* the unexpected! This means that all of us (not just leaders) should be praying consistently and in a focused manner. As we pray and put things in order in our lives and in our churches, we can prepare for the blessing that *will* come.

DOCTRINAL AND LITURGICAL DIFFERENCES, RELIGIOUS ELITISM AND EXCLUSIVITY

Based on our limited background and experience, we often have emotional knee-jerk reactions to doctrinal or liturgical differences in others. Perhaps it is just preaching style, form, or emphasis, but our reflex reaction is frequently, "It's different; I don't like it. It's wrong!" We start finding fault and pigeonholing others. I have done this myself when I found the rituals of another church were unfamiliar. With the reckless enthusiasm of youth, I acted like a partisan bull in a denominational china shop, causing unnecessary injury to the sensitivities of others.

All too often we submit to the widespread fear that to brush up against the divergent attitudes of other Christians will compromise the beliefs we hold dear. *We put ourselves into neat little confessional boxes, each with its own label! And the Divine Trademark, "Love one another" gets completely detached.* When we allow our opinions or traditions to get in the way of God's all-consuming love, we block the blessing He wants to pour out on His whole Church. God works in ways that transcend our intellect and religious expectations. According to Jesus, if an issue is not understandable to a small child, it is not important as an entry criterion to the Kingdom of Heaven (see Matt. 18:3; Mark 10:15). We would do well to accept this.

Religious Elitism Divides

Paul states that "knowledge puffs up, but love builds up" (1 Cor. 8:1). Sadly, religious elitism, usually based on theological (mis)understanding, is present in many different churches and denominations. Some consider they have the truth because they know the Word and can quote Bible and verse on almost any issue you care to mention. Others disdain those who have not received a "second blessing" through the Baptism of the Holy Spirit. Water baptism, over the centuries, has been the occasion for martyrdom in the battle between those who practice infant baptism and others who baptize believing adults. I even know one group of Christians which refuses to meet with other believers because "the others" do not pray in the same way!

To a large extent, our doctrinal and liturgical standpoints result from the experiences that have formed us. Few of us objectively evaluate our accumulated training to gain a balanced opinion. We may differ, not because either is right or wrong, but because we are accustomed to different spiritual and social cultures. In this way, *our denominational bickering may have more in common with social discrimination than with spiritual understanding.* As with social integration, we should be willing to learn from one another. We can then take a big step toward the restoration of unity with fellow believers.

Jesus Himself emphasized that maintaining interpersonal contact is more important than religious doctrine. He admonished the Pharisees for allowing their observance of traditions to damage even their relationships with their parents (see Matt. 15:3-9). The lesson is clear—do not let religion replace relationship. These days, when challenged by doctrinal differences among believers, I try to keep my mouth shut and ask the Holy Spirit to show me how to be more gracious. Usually, He reveals that many of my concerns are very minor in comparison with the joy of family ties.

Apparently Insurmountable Differences

Some differences between Christians, admittedly, are difficult to bridge. When the place of a specific denominational tradition or of a church leader is given priority over the fellowship of believers, there is often little room for maneuver. Here it is important to emphasize that *we should stand up for what we believe to be the truth!* We should not be weak and easily swayed; neither should we ignore, judge, or ostracize another believer even when it proves difficult to reconcile our differences. The only practical approach, without crossing the boundaries of our own basis of belief, is to graciously respect the standpoint of the other believer. In some cases, as we considered in Chapter 2, it may be necessary to take different directions.

It requires courage and maturity to remove our doctrinal or theological straitjackets and actively seek communication with believers who have different traditions or theology. We may be derided by those in our own denomination, but the Lord certainly approves of our attempts to build bridges.

The challenge is not to search initially for common theological ground, but to make a determined effort to build friendships. In this respect, it is best to try to find a common language. We have lived in several different countries and learned four different languages. Each time we have moved, the people we got to know initially were those with whom we shared a spoken language, and they often became long-lasting friends. Finding a common denominator creates a basis for respecting alternative viewpoints. Seeds of friendship grow into strong bonds of love but only if we give them the chance to germinate and grow.

The common denominator may be music, children, a hobby, sport, or shared community concern. Often it lies outside the confines of the local church building, in a school parents' association, on a garden allotment, or on a football pitch. Enjoying the shared activity, we can discover common areas of personal testimony or topics of special interest. It is tragic if we deny ourselves these opportunities for mutual upbuilding by remaining isolated in our religious ivory towers.

In this respect, the Lausanne Covenant—agreed upon at the first Conference on World Evangelization in 1974 by 2,300 people from 150 nations, reaffirmed at the second conference in Manila in 1989, and again at the recent third conference, held in Cape Town in October 2010—is a valuable basis for collaboration among Protestant evangelicals.[5] It emphasizes the need to evangelize not just in word but also in deed. It places the verbal communication of the message of salvation and active social concern on an equal footing and encourages believers to work together to spread the righteousness of the Kingdom of God in a way that changes lives personally and socially. It is certainly worth turning to this covenant as a reference point in dealing with potential areas of difference. In every joint Christian endeavor, let us seek to find *first* the common ground on which we agree. This is often broader than we expect!

Avoid Putting Leaders on a Pedestal

All of us, leaders in particular, need interactions with other Christians to sharpen us and keep us balanced (see Prov. 27:17). The elevation of church leaders and the tendency of some to promote subjective interpretations of God's Word has been a constant source of division in the Church. When the leaders of a church become elitist, isolating themselves from other groups, the inevitable result is an inordinate sense of their own importance. They start giving themselves names and titles, demand increased obedience by their members, and introduce restrictive practices. Sooner or later, the church is in danger of splitting, becoming a sect, or simply collapsing.

Sadly, we have seen this happen to a church we used to attend. As members we learned a lot, particularly about evangelism. But the emphasis placed on submission to leadership led to a loss of accountability and, ultimately, the expulsion of the leader, who had resorted to cheating to maintain his position.

As in the business world, so in the Church a plurality of leaders aids a balanced approach to leadership. Humble acceptance of our limitations is also crucial. After healing a lame man, Paul admonished the crowds in Lystra for their adulation of him and Barnabas as gods (see Acts 14:8-18). And Peter did not consider it beneath his dignity to visit Cornelius, a Roman centurion, in complete contravention of Jewish tradition, with its strict separation of Jews and Gentiles in matters of worship and lifestyle (see Acts 10:1-48). Jesus Himself was at pains to give glory to His Father. When called "good teacher" by a questioner, Jesus pointed out that "no-one is good—except God alone" (Mark 10:18). He made it clear that to be a spiritual leader, we have to become "the servant of all" (Mark 9:35), a position He underlined by washing His disciples' feet and dying for us on a criminal's cross. As church members, we have a responsibility not only to pray for our leaders, but to encourage them, perhaps with challenging words.

JUDGMENTALISM

Jesus was very angry with religious hypocrisy and pretence. This is also a major barrier to the unity of Christians. We all have weak areas beneath our pedestals, but are we willing to admit it? We prefer to make ourselves look better than we actually are. This not only raises a barrier between us, but also prevents the Holy Spirit from cleaning up our lives.

Harsh Criticism Is Common and Destructive

It is easy to point the finger at a fellow believer who has a splinter in his eye and not notice the huge plank in our own! (See Matthew 7:1-5.) Jesus shows through this parable that He considers the sin of judgmentalism to be worse than the fault that evokes it! Repeatedly in the New Testament, we are warned not to judge one another (see James 4:11-12; Rom. 14:13). As the nineteenth-century American Methodist evangelist George D. Watson pointed out, it is a universal law that when we judge others, we naturally do so harshly, placing the worst construction on what we see or hear.[6] Jumping to the wrong conclusions and defending our own points of view, we become argumentative, critical, and slanderous.

Using the same tongue with which we praise the Lord, we attack our fellow believers, instead of praying for, encouraging, and supporting them. As a result, we mess up our relationship with the Lord:

> *...anyone who is so much as angry with a brother or sister is guilty of murder. Carelessly call a brother "idiot!" and you just might find yourself hauled into court. Thoughtlessly yell "stupid!" at a sister and you are on the brink of hellfire. The simple moral fact is that words kill* (Matthew 5:21-22 TM).

A relative of mine recently sent me a brief story, which illustrates how careful we need to be to avoid criticism. A young couple moved into a new neighborhood. While eating breakfast, the woman saw her neighbor hanging her washing outside. "That laundry is not very clean," she said. "She does not know how to wash correctly. She needs better soap powder." Her husband looked on, but remained silent. Every time her neighbor hung out her washing, the young woman made the same comment. A month later, the woman was surprised to see a line of clean washing and said to her husband, "Look, she has learned how to wash correctly. I wonder who taught her?" The husband said, "I got up early this morning and cleaned our windows!" What we see in others depends on the purity of the window we look through.

Jesus said, "Every kingdom divided against itself will be ruined" (Matt. 12:25). By the same token, each word we utter in judgment against our fellow believers will damage the Kingdom of God. By harshly criticizing fellow Christians, we are tearing down living stones, ones that we ourselves may have been working to build up. Paul warns his pupil, Timothy, "The Lord's servant must not quarrel; instead, he must be kind to everyone, able to teach, not resentful" (2 Tim. 2:24). How many bridges would be restored between Christians with differing opinions if Paul's warning were more carefully heeded?

Exhort Rather Than Condemn

In comparison to the number of times in the New Testament where we are charged to love, forgive, and be gracious and merciful, there are few passages censuring Christian behavior. These are generally admonitions to church leaders to be concerned for the welfare of believers under their care. Jesus' presentation of God's standards for wealth and possessions (see Mark 10:21-27); sexual morality (see Matt. 5:27-28); and forbearance (see Matt. 5:38-42) seem unattainably high. But His practical application of these standards was gracious and understanding. Jesus deliberately avoided condemning the rich young man for his enjoyment of wealth (see Mark 10:17-23); Zacchaeus for his greed (see Luke 19:1-10); the Samaritan woman for her immorality (see John 4:17-19); Thomas for his doubts (see John 20:27); or Peter for his denial (see John 21:15-17). Rather than condemning them, He encouraged them to improve their lives and behavior in God's strength.

Paul too challenged churches, not to make them feel badly about their behavior, but to prevent them from spoiling their relationships with the Lord and each another. His main criticism of the Corinthians was that their behavior was breaking down their own unity, through divisive arguments and quarrels (see 1 Cor. 1:10-13; 3:1-4; 11:18; 2 Cor. 12:20); lawsuits (see 1 Cor. 6:7);

sexual immorality (see 1 Cor. 6:12-18); selfish behavior at agape love feasts (see 1 Cor. 11:20-21); disorderly services (see 1 Cor. 14:39-40); and unjustified grudges (see 2 Cor. 6:12; 12:19). Even so, this was not simply accusatory criticism from Paul. He knew that consistent, willful refusal to change such behavior was not in keeping with the fact that our bodies are temples of the Holy Spirit (see 1 Cor. 6:19). On the one hand, Paul challenged the Galatians for being legalistic and called them to live in freedom through the Holy Spirit (see Gal. 1:8-9; 3:1-5; 5:22-23). On the other hand, he commended the Thessalonians for their faith (see 1 Thess. 1:3) and the Corinthians for their generosity (see 2 Cor. 8:10). He encouraged the Philippians to continue in humility (see Phil. 2:1-11) and the Romans to be considerate toward the weak (see Rom. 15:1). Paul reminded the Ephesians that rather than being judgmental and critical, they had a more important "calling" to be humble, patient, and to bear with each other in love (see Eph. 4:1-2).

Let us avoid criticizing others for breaking petty rules that we ourselves are barely able to keep; instead, let us encourage one another to aim at a higher goal. How about looking to other churches for ideas for growth and outreach? Perhaps we can find among them possibilities and friendships which have eluded us, but will enrich the life of our church.

The Highest Goal

The Kingdom of God, which we should be promoting as our primary goal (see Matt. 6:33), is found within the lives of people who love the Lord Jesus (see Luke 17:20-21) and who want to reveal more of His righteousness to others. This Kingdom is not "passing judgment on one another," but "righteousness, peace and joy in the Holy Spirit" (see Rom. 14:13,17).

Jesus refused to defend Himself against any of the accusations of religious heresy or sedition that were leveled against Him, except to witness to the fact that He was the King of the Jews, the Son of

God (see Matt. 27:11-14; Luke 22:66–23:10). The other issues were not worth dying for. It was as the Son of God that Jesus died, not for any secondary accusation. The bottom line for us is that only Jesus and our love for fellow believers are worth dying for, not doctrine and theology.

ENDNOTES

1. http://www.lyricsfreak.com/k/keith+green/asleep+in+the+light_20077341.html.

2. Andrew Murray, *Reaching Your World for Christ* (New Kensington, PA: Whitaker House, 1997), 42.

3. Jim Cymbala, *Fresh Wind, Fresh Fire* (Grand Rapids, MI: Zondervan, 1997), 139.

4. Cymbala, *Fresh Wind, Fresh Fire*, 145.

5. http://www.lausanne.org/en/documents/lausanne covenant.html.

6. George D. Watson, in *A Pot of Oil*, quoted by Paul E. Billheimer, *Love Covers*, 157.

CHAPTER 7

RESTORING UNITY

...HE [GOD] CARES ONLY FOR TEMPLES BUILDING
AND NOT FOR TEMPLES BUILT.

—C.S. Lewis, English author,
1898–1963, in *Surprised by Joy*

The face of Zagreb has been changing rapidly. Fashionable shopping malls and well-stocked supermarkets are replacing the old-fashioned corner shops. The crumbling facades of once stately buildings also have been undergoing a transformation. The ornate gables are being restored, and the old, discolored plaster now gleams with fresh paint in the hot summer sun. But before reappearing, the buildings were hidden for months behind scaffolding and advertising billboards. The only signs of what was going on behind were the occasional dust clouds from power tools and the banging of hammers. Like any repair task, the renovation could only start once the old decrepit layers of dirt and grime had been removed. The same principle applies to maintaining our relationships with other Christians.

109

Confession and Repentance

Once obstacles to unity have been identified, we must admit and repent of them: "If we confess our sins, He is faithful and just and will forgive us our sins and purify us from all unrighteousness" (1 John 1:9). I believe there is a widespread misunderstanding of confession. It is not a religious process of humiliation—God's way of making us feel miserable about what we have done wrong. James puts it this way: "Therefore confess your sins to each other and pray for each other so that you may be healed" (James 5:16). Simply put, God wants to heal us, emotionally, spiritually, and physically, through humble confession of our sin, prayer for one another, and the consequent receipt of God's forgiveness. There is no benefit either to God or to us if the Body of Christ on this earth is going around feeling sorry for herself! This is not the picture of the victorious Church that Jesus died to establish.

Contrition *precedes* and rapidly makes place for confession as we recognize and in our hearts accept that we have sinned. Then at the moment we confess with our mouths what we have believed in our hearts, we receive the forgiveness and justification God has promised through Jesus (see Rom. 10:7-10). He "richly blesses all who call on Him" (Rom. 10:12). This for me is one of the wonders of Jesus' work of salvation. By faith and through confession with our mouths, we receive immediate forgiveness and purification from our sins on account of Christ's work for us (see 1 John 1:9). And this applies to our relationships with God both individually and corporately as members of the Body. As Paul says, "If one part suffers, every part suffers with it" (1 Cor. 12:26). So the sooner we confess our sins against the unity of the Body, the sooner the Body will be healed. This is what Paul describes as living "a life worthy of the calling" (Eph. 4:1).

In my view, we seem to be schizophrenic. We ask God to deal with our own personal needs and those of our families and friends, but completely overlook the fact that Jesus is hurting from extensive injuries to His whole Body. We try to find a plaster to bind a cut on our little finger, when both legs and an arm are broken! The lost wonder of the Church is that when we start to fix the major injuries causing disunity, the little individual scratches of interpersonal differences are often healed spontaneously as God pours out His blessing in response to our restored unity! "If one part is honoured, every part rejoices with it" (1 Cor. 12:26).

Clearing the Highway

One of the verses God gave us for Zagreb is "pass through the gates! Prepare the way for the people…Build up the highway! Remove the stones" (Isa. 62:10). God has created an open door into this city to build His Kingdom. But in order to enter, the stones that stand in the way need to be removed. These are the obstacles between us, as we discussed in the previous chapter, which must be confessed to one another. Confession will open the gate, not only in Zagreb, but wherever the Church of God is in disrepair.

Talking of thoroughfares, Zagreb roads are not one of its plus points. The asphalt is uneven from repeated repair, and sunken manhole covers lie in wait to assault the front tires of my car. And as though these hindrances were insufficient inducement to drive slowly, the local council has added speed bumps at regular intervals! I try to avoid certain roads just to protect my car.

The same is true of our relationships with believers. Where the issues are still sensitive, we tend to avoid the "bumps," so problems do not get addressed. This does not aid our unity at all. Recently, the Zagreb city council started resurfacing some major roads, leveling off the manhole covers, and making the driving experience smoother. The same is true with the relational pathways between members of the Church. We benefit individually and corporately if we address the issues rather than avoiding them.

Do Not Delay

The Lord wants His Body to be fit, healthy, and united. Consequently, confessing and clearing hindrances should be as natural and simple as washing our hands, which we do several times every day. Although James encourages us to "confess [our] sins to each other and pray for each other" (James 5:16), this does not mean that we have to keep recounting all our sins. It does not strengthen a marriage relationship to tell your partner continually everything you do wrong; rather, the stuff that is adversely affecting the relationship needs to be addressed. Whatever negative concerns come to mind when we think about other believers or fellowships need to be attended to.

The sooner we deal with these issues, the less the damage to the relationships. In urging the Ephesian Christians to maintain their unity, Paul also warns them to put things right with an angered brother the same day (see Eph. 4:26). And Jesus cautions that we should be reconciled with an offended brother before we attempt to bring any sort of offering to God (see Matt. 5:23-24). Otherwise, instead of being pleasant to God, our worship and service is tainted (see Isa. 43:24). God will not accept our sacrifices of prayer and "powerful worship" if we are deliberately harboring anger or bitterness toward each other.

Long-Standing Problems

Some things, though, particularly between churches, have been obstacles for so long, they no longer occur to us. In Second Kings 18:4 we read about King Hezekiah destroying the bronze serpent that Moses had made in the desert, centuries previously. At first, it had been the God-given means to heal anyone who looked at it from the snake bites they had received. By Hezekiah's time, it had become a tradition and a problem, as it was being worshiped instead of God.

What traditional bronze serpents do we have? Which skeletons have been hiding in our cupboards? What do we need to confess and remove? What barriers between churches or denominations, erected centuries ago, continue to govern our disturbed relationships? *Their unconfessed presence is an open wound in the flesh of the Church and a hindrance to the blessing that God wants to release.*

A reconciliation meeting was held in the early 1990s in Northern Ireland, when members of the Irish Republican Army, Roman Catholic organizations, Protestant police, and British army representatives came together to confess their mutual aggression and ask for forgiveness for the "troubles" of the previous twenty-five years. One wonders to what extent this meeting contributed to the subsequent successful establishment of a government of unity, across sectarian lines, in Northern Ireland.

Not all of us are called to build bridges at such a wide-ranging level. We should start first with the relationships closest to home. What about damaged relationships in our own church or biological family? What about the people we avoid because of harsh words that were exchanged or because we disagreed with their theology? Many divisions are not even over theological issues. They are the result of personal animosities or family disagreements that arose years ago and are perpetuated by gossip and criticism. Negative attitudes build up over generations, as family or national feuds became more entrenched, and are frequently carried over into disagreements between churches and denominations. Many of the opinions we hold are not really our own. We have just "inherited" and mentally embellished them through the biased attitudes of our predecessors. These issues must be addressed within the Church of God! If we want the blessing, then we need to repair the damage. Let us confess our sins to one another so that God can heal the wounds.

Humility and Repentance

Having recognized the obstacles, we are often too proud to deal with them! It is time to follow Christ's example and humbly acknowledge that there have been errors on both sides. Something that happened over thirty years ago has remained in my memory as a wonderful example of humility and willingness to restore right relationships.

At the time, we attended a Pentecostal church in Holland. One of the deacons was a man in his fifties with two adult children. The whole family was highly respected and loved throughout the church. One evening at a prayer meeting, the father stood up and offered aloud a prayer of confession. I cannot remember what the issue was, but I will never forget the image of this tearful, respected man, humbly and publicly confessing his weakness before the church. In my eyes, his standing increased immensely. Not only were he and his loving family exemplary by what they did, but his humility and willingness to free his life of anything that would limit the Holy Spirit spoke volumes. If only we were all as willing!

But confession alone is insufficient. We have to turn around and start acting differently. We need to repent:

> *If My people, who are called by My name, will humble themselves and pray and seek My face and turn from their wicked ways, then will I hear from heaven and will forgive their sin and will heal their land* (2 Chronicles 7:14).

Where we as believers have taken separate ways, paved with judgmentalism, pride, and lack of love, we should seek paths we can walk together. The obvious place to start is in our families. Are we prepared to accept responsibility and start talking to an offended relative, even if they are at fault? Then, in our churches, when did we last speak to a member with whom we had a difference of opinion? It can also be a very rewarding experience to deliberately seek contact with members of another fellowship which broke away from your own at some time in the past. You may be surprised to find how pleasant they are and end up making new friends.

FORGIVENESS—REAPPLYING THE GLUE

Kindness, compassion, and forgiveness should be the natural hallmarks of a Christian, "just as in Christ God forgave you" (Eph. 4:32). When Peter asked Jesus whether he should forgive his brother seven times, Jesus responded that he should forgive seventy-seven times (see Matt. 18:22). I realize that seventy-seven is a symbolic number, but if we assume that most people sleep eight hours a night, leaving fourteen waking hours each day, to forgive someone seventy-seven times in one day means forgiving every eleven minutes. In other words, forgiving a fellow believer should be the automatic response of the Spirit-filled character. While confession and repentance involve recognizing and removing the dirt that has caused the parts to separate, forgiveness reapplies a new layer of adhesive love.

Cleaning Our Own Hallway

The pastor of a church we once attended and his wife were both quite temperamental characters. They admitted to having intense "dynamic discussions!" But the wife said she really appreciated the outcome of these arguments. Once they made up and forgave each other, their love for one another was greater than before their quarrel! This beneficial outcome of forgiveness between Christians is guaranteed, whatever the division that needs repairing.

Forgiveness provides greater benefit to the forgiver than to the one who has been forgiven. If we forgive others, God forgives us (see Matt. 6:14). The enemy, on the other hand, taking advantage of our pride, tries to convince us that to forgive someone who has wronged us is a sign of weakness. But it is *always* the right thing to clear the channels of communication between ourselves, the Lord, and our fellow Christians. And it is usually easier for the one who has been least wronged to take the first step toward reconciliation. Unless we clean the entrance to our homes, no matter how often we clean the living room, every time we enter the house we walk the dirt back into the room. It is much more logical to wipe your shoes at the doorstep, clean the hallway, and keep the rest of the house clean! Unforgiveness leaves dirty footprints all over our lives and those of others; bending our knees to apply forgiveness has far-reaching effects.

Tearing Down Fortresses

How many of us carry hurts around in our hearts? You are the one who suffers—not the one you do not forgive! The enemy is a master builder of mental castles, alien fortresses, and strongholds of antipathy, particularly toward those who should be closest and most dear to us. Such devilish defenses should be attacked with the weapons of prayer and Scripture, because these spiritual weapons "have divine power to demolish strongholds…arguments and every pretension that sets itself up against the knowledge of God" (2 Cor. 10:4-5). When we have the humility and courage to address these barriers in God's strength and seek reconciliation, the fortresses collapse like a house of cards.

It is not "honorable" to defend the family or church reputation over a long-standing disagreement. It is cowardly because we do not have the courage to seek restoration. To forgive is the pathway of courage, strength, and peace. Just look at the benefit that has accrued for the people of South Africa because one man—Nelson Mandela—was willing to forgive his racist oppressors for 28 years of imprisonment. As president, he and Archbishop Desmond Tutu led the way in introducing reconciliation to the whole country.

Forgiveness is the unavoidable gate into the city of unity and the blessing of restoration that God longs to share with us. How can we pray for God to pour out His Spirit on our church? How can we ask God to answer our prayers? How can we expect His blessing on our work for Him when we hold grudges against each other, when we avoid those we do not like, or when we cling to old prejudices from generations past? By humbly forgiving others, we draw closer to God, and He draws closer to us (see James 4: 8).

I love football! I quickly developed a liking for the Croatian style when the national team finished third in the World Cup in 1998, having thrashed one of the favorites, Germany, 3-0 in the quarter final! Ten years later, during the European Cup in Austria/Switzerland, Croatia again beat Germany 2-1, finishing top of their qualifying group! The team had played some dazzling football, so when they met Turkey in the quarter finals everyone expected a fireworks display of Mediterranean footballing flair! But instead of fireworks, the match just glimmered. Croatia was overcautious and lacked confidence when presented with goal-scoring opportunities. With Croatia leading, Turkey remarkably equalized in extra time and confidently clinched the game in a penalty shoot-out. Rather than facing up to the challenge with confidence, as in the previous round, Croatia allowed nervousness to creep in and squandered their chances.

For too long the enemy has convinced many Christians that we cannot overcome the obstacles in our lives. We assume that the barriers between us are unfortunate but unchangeable. These are lies that are damaging the unity and function of the whole Church! The opposite is true, we *have* to courageously remove these obstacles, in God's strength, to be able to grow more like Jesus!

Back to Basics

In practice, it is most effective to start on the basis of our mutual relationship in Christ. This is the basis of our unity, not the various doctrines we hold. I believe a crucial issue is the means by which we start our relationship with God. For the Roman Catholic, this is by the sacrament of baptism, and for the Anglican by christening and confirmation. For the Reformed Protestant, it is usually the spoken prayer of repentance and the experience of being born again. And the charismatic Pentecostal will want to add that the baptism in the Holy Spirit is an important further step. Without commenting on their relative importance, I believe that none of these initial steps has any lasting worth unless the result is an evident, experiential relationship with the living Christ and a deep desire to serve and live for Him. It is this relationship that is then recognizable, as Jesus said, by our love for Him and expressed in our love for one another. If this is not our personal testimony as Christians, then all our doctrine, theology, and tradition is just window dressing and of little eternal spiritual value. When we can mutually recognize the "family likeness" in the loving lives of our fellow believers, we have a basis for unity. This will need care and attention, as in any relationship. If we accept the fact *that* we are family is more important than *how* we joined the family, I believe there will be much more opportunity to live together for the glory of God. We can then start building on this foundation.

Repairing the Broken Walls

The ancient Israelites thought that by going through the motions of standard rituals, they were following the Divine Builder's instructions. Speaking through the prophet Isaiah, God tells the people why He has not responded to their apparently correct approach to fasting. He explains that He cannot respond when they are exploiting their workers, breaking their fasts with arguments, and hitting out at each other. He says that the fasting He wants to see is the removal of injustice, care for the poor, and provision for their "own flesh and blood." Under these conditions, God promises that "healing will quickly appear" (Isa. 58:8).

> *...If you do away with the yoke of oppression, with the pointing finger and malicious talk, and if you spend yourselves in behalf of the hungry and satisfy the needs of the oppressed, then your light will rise in the darkness, and your night will become like the noonday. The Lord will guide you always; He will satisfy your needs in a sun-scorched land and will strengthen your frame. You will be like a well-watered garden, like a spring whose waters never fail. Your people will rebuild the ancient ruins and will raise up the age-old foundations; you will be called Repairer of Broken Walls, Restorer of Streets with Dwellings (Isaiah 58:9-12).*

God's Word never changes. His promises remain as applicable today as they were thousands of years ago. It is time to start rebuilding the broken walls of His Church! Not with rules, ritual, and rancor, but with care, consideration, and charity—and this applies to every believer, whatever our circumstances.

SEEK PEACE

The stretch of land between the rivers Sava and Drava in the east and the Adriatic Sea to the west has been a theatre of unrest and dispute for many centuries. Croatia—like several other East European countries—has seen brother turn against brother many times in its turbulent past. This started with the incursion of the Central European Slavic peoples in the seventh and eighth centuries, through the centuries of Hungarian and Austrian domination, when Croatia was the Habsburg barrier against the marauding Ottoman Turks, up to the social unrest of the mid-nineteenth century. The fratricide continued with the rollercoaster of allegiances in the twentieth century, annexation by Nazi Germany, and takeover by the communist partisans under Tito, culminating in the repulsion of the Serbian invasion following the declaration of independence in 1991.

Croatia's capital, Zagreb, received a Royal Charter from the King of Hungary in 1292 as a free market, in gratitude for the protection the city gave him from the Tartar armies from the East. The city was created as a haven of hospitality and trade for all the surrounding peoples, as reflected in its coat-of-arms with an open gate. But here too division took its toll. The civil center, Gradec, was locked in regular armed dispute with the ecclesiastical center, Kaptol. The blood shed as these two rivals collided is documented in the name of the connecting bridge (now a street), the *Krvavi Most*, which translates as "Bloody Bridge." The open door still remains, with the age-old invitation to unite in peace, a prospect that challenges us as Christians to pray together that the mercy, justice, and righteousness of God will take command through His united people.

The State of Shalom

As Christian believers, we are united already by the cross of Christ:

> *For He Himself is our peace, who…has destroyed…the dividing wall of hostility, by abolishing in His flesh the law…to create in Himself one new man out of the two, thus making peace, and in this one body to reconcile both*

of them to God through the cross, by which He put to death their hostility (Ephesians 2:14-16).

Paul says that through the cross Christ made peace, putting to death the hostility which separated Jews and Gentiles and everyone else who may previously have been disunited for whatever reason. He came to pull down the dividing wall between us. The resulting spiritual reality is that we are one Body, through one Spirit and one faith (see Eph. 4:4-5). We are charged to keep the unity of the Spirit in the bond of peace (see Eph. 4:3). And it is this peace we are encouraged to sustain (see 1 Pet. 3:11).

Peace through the cross involves actively working for the good of others, a peace worth negotiating, securing, and protecting. It is a peace that requires us to speak considerately of one another, that demands mutual respect and prayerful concern (see 1 Pet. 3:10-12). This peace is one we should be prepared to suffer for, courageously defend, and honor (see 1 Pet. 3:13-16). It is not an environment in which all think or do the same, nor is it achievable only when all Christian groups reach agreement on doctrines or procedures. But it involves the deliberate arbitration of potential conflict; praying and working toward a state of physical, emotional, spiritual, and social wholeness among believers; caring for each others' well-being and happiness; and finding our strength in the joy of the Lord—a condition in which mutual respect and support contribute to provide lives of calm and tranquillity, the true *shalom*.

Evelyn Beatrice Hall, an English writer at the beginning of the twentieth century, famously described the philosophy of Voltaire in this way: "I disapprove of what you say, but I will defend to the death your right to say it."[1] If we as Christians were more gracious toward one another, respecting our differences but supporting one another unflinchingly in our faith, peace would have greater freedom to reign.

Paul actively sought to promote peace as he urged the leaders of the church in Philippi to mediate for him between Euodia and Syntyche (see Phil. 4:2). Significantly, he does not address the rights and wrongs of their disagreement but urges them to get back into a right relationship with each other. Peter says that we are to "live in harmony with one another," repaying evil with blessing "so that you may inherit a blessing" (1 Pet. 3:8-9). Here again, as in Psalm 133:1-3, living in harmony with one another and seeking peace is a *prerequisite* for God's blessing. If we invest in words and acts of peace and love, then it works to our own good. Part of the inheritance gained is a greater blessing from God.

Sowing Seeds of Peace

If we are to see our churches work in unity and righteousness spread throughout our secular societies, then we need to be peacemakers. As we sow in peace we shall raise a harvest of righteousness (see James 3:18). For the seed of the Kingdom of God to produce a bountiful harvest, however, the conditions for sowing, watering, and harvesting have to be optimal. The better the conditions, the bigger the harvest.

The farmer needs to sow seed undisturbed by disputes with his neighbors or unrest among his workers. The climate should not be too harsh so the grain can grow without being buffeted by heavy winds and hailstorms. And, as we considered in an earlier chapter, the harvesters should work in a coordinated and efficient manner. Unity in the bond of peace is the ideal climate for righteousness to grow, and "righteousness exalts a nation" (Prov. 14:34). Not only will the peace made through the unity of believers bring blessing to the Church, but it will inevitably overflow to bless the society around us, just as the unity practiced by the early church led to awe and favor among the citizens of Jerusalem (see Acts 2:43-47).

I have been privileged to see this happen, in a limited way, in the workplace. When I first started working in Zagreb, there were strong animosities among some of my colleagues. At times my patience ran thin as well! But believing it was best not to get involved in these quarrels, I sought to build bridges and make peace at least between me and them. One particularly difficult colleague eventually became a friend and came to me for advice on a number of matters. Shortly before I left, a number of people wanted to know what I believed.

My boss even admitted he was jealous of my faith, and I had opportunities to pray with others.

These small, personal illustrations help to show that the example we set, either as individuals or as a group of Christians, has wide-ranging effects on people around us. By sowing peace in the working environment, I believe everyone benefits. When our company, under threat of closure, was rescued through acquisition by a large company, at least two senior colleagues suggested that perhaps God was in control after all!

Our workplace, school, or university is an ideal place to experience the benefits of maintaining Christian unity in the bond of peace. We are often thrown together with a variety of colleagues or students, including believers of various shades. The students' Christian Union is a marvelous melting-pot for open-minded Christians. As we meet, share, pray, and work together, we learn to respect different points of view. We leave lasting impressions of how Christians can get on with each other (or not!) on the silent, unbelieving observers around us. In addition, lifelong friendships can result among Christians we may otherwise never have met.

Sowing seeds of peace among fellow believers, then, can have long-lasting, mutual benefits for our own relationships and for those of people in our immediate environment. But God wants the blessing on His united people to spread much wider.

Joint Prayer for Prosperity

When the nation of Judah was heading into exile in Babylonia, Jeremiah prophesied, "Seek the peace and prosperity of the city to which I have carried you into exile. Pray to the Lord for it, because if it prospers, you too will prosper" (Jer. 29:7). As foreigners or "exiles" in Zagreb, we have made it our goal to pray for the city—its leaders and ministries, its institutions and businesses—that justice and righteousness will flow through every part. And we encourage other Christians to work and pray for the blessing and prosperity of Zagreb's inhabitants.

Wherever we live, our calling as Christians is to unite together in love, and to work and pray for the peace of the town or city to which we have been sent. This is a goal we can all share, a vision which gives us a common purpose, irrespective of our differences. Each of us has something we can do, at work, in our neighborhood, through our local church or fellowship. Each church has its area of influence, its specific ministries or emphases. And as we shall see in the last chapter, these can complement one another to provide a patchwork quilt of blessing that covers the whole city.

Expectant, Corporate Prayer Is Needed

The command of God through Jeremiah to the exiles of Judah was to pray for the city. Expectant, believing, focused corporate prayer changes everything! If we humble ourselves and pray together, God will hear and heal our land, as He told Solomon (see 2 Chron. 7:13-14). This united prayer, God promises, will bring prosperity to the city. He will respond to our prayers, forgive the people, and pour rain onto the dry ground.

Believing, corporate prayer and praise was the prelude to the outpouring of the Holy Spirit in power and caused buildings to shake (see Acts 1:14; Acts 4:31). Such prayer moved the hand of God to open prison doors and to tear off chains (see Acts 16:25-26). This prayer releases wisdom to rulers and peace to the country, enables the Holy Spirit to channel authority to leaders to establish churches, and brings healing to the sick (see 1 Tim. 2:1-2; Acts 13:3; Acts 14:23; James 5:14-15). It is always effective for all occasions, all needs, and all believers (see Eph. 6:18). It is prayer that is shared by the Savior (see John 17:8-26) and that is poured out as incense in the throne room of Heaven (see Rev. 5:8). When we unite in our role as priests to God and offer prayer and praise in keeping with His will, we change the course of history and eternity.

We do not have because we do not ask God (see James 4:2). As Andrew Murray observed,

> *It is high time for the church to stop looking at prayer only in the light of our feebleness or our limited desires. We must begin to believe that God, in the mystery of prayer, has entrusted us with a force that can move the heavenly world and bring its power down to this earth.*[2]

May God help us to be peacemakers, representatives imbued with power from on high who are rightly called "sons of God" (Matt. 5:9).

ENDNOTES

1. http://en.wikipedia.org/wiki/Evelyn_Beatrice_Hall#cite_note-1.

2. Andrew Murray, *Reaching Your World for Christ*, 107.

CHAPTER 8

THE TASTE OF NEW WINE

ONE NOT ONLY DRINKS THE WINE,
ONE SMELLS IT, OBSERVES IT, TASTES IT,
SIPS IT AND ONE TALKS ABOUT IT.

—King Edward VII of England,
1841–1910

Unity grows when it is nurtured in the right environment and when the various components blend together in harmonious combination, just like a good wine. Despite injunctions in both the Old and New Testaments to avoid drunkenness, fully-laden vines were widely recognized as signs of God's blessing. The beautiful grapes of Canaan were praised by the spies that Joshua sent to assess the quality of the land (see Num. 13:23-24, 27). New wine was to be offered to the Lord and drunk as part of the celebrations of thankfulness for God's goodness (see Deut. 14:22-26). The psalmist thanked God for the wine "that gladdens the heart of man" (Ps. 104:15), and Jesus Himself chose to perform His first miracle by converting water into exquisite wine at the wedding in Cana (see John 2:1-11). So wine can be seen as an illustration of the outworking of God's blessing poured out in response to brothers living together in unity (see Ps. 133:3).

To produce a good wine, a great deal of care and attention must be paid to the growing conditions, harvesting, fermenting, and the final maturation in containers. Like a good wine, unity between Christians cannot be maintained just by throwing the constituent parts into a container. The enjoyment, satisfaction, and blessing we and others gain from practicing and celebrating our unity result from procedures such as pruning, blending, crushing, and bottling. The process is challenging, but the end results are a delight to both the spiritual and physical senses!

THE VINE AND ITS BRANCHES

Jesus called Himself the True Vine and His disciples the branches that bear the grapes (see John 15:1-2). Only by remaining attached to the vine can branches bear fruit, and only by remaining in close communication with the Lord can we, as Christians, expect to be able to bear fruit in our lives—the visible expression of life (see John 15:4).

Together in the Vine

In spring, the tree-covered hills around Zagreb turn white with blossom. Then in autumn, on south-facing areas, juicy bunches of grapes hang enticingly from the branches of the vines. We frequently walk in the countryside, but rarely would we say, "Look at that beautiful branch!" A much more likely exclamation would be, "Look at the beautiful blossom on that tree!" or "That vine has a lot of grapes!" Individual branches rarely stand out as particularly attractive, but, all together, the branches, leaves, flowers, and fruit reflect the beauty of the whole plant.

In the same way, we as branches on the True Vine, exist not primarily for our own benefit, but so that *together* we can live "for the praise of His glory" (Eph. 1:12). This is the highest calling we have as believing Christians. We do not have to justify our individual existence by showing off our knowledge and achievements, but living together in harmony with other believers, our complementary lives, fruit, and actions should provoke the onlooker to respond, "God is wonderful!" (see Matt. 5:16).

It is essential that branches not only stay attached to the vine, but remain together. It is the concentration of fruit, growing from the same strain of vine, planted in the same soil, and exposed to the same sunlight that ultimately leads to a tasteful wine of constant quality. Jesus prayed to His Father that His followers might "be one as We [Jesus and the Father] are one: I in them and You in Me" (John 17:22-23). *This complex, intimate communion between the Father, the Son, His disciples, and one another then results in the beautiful demonstration to the watching world of the love of God for mankind* (see John 17:23). Jesus was only able to reveal the love of the Father for thirty-three short years. But through the presence and power of the Holy Spirit, we are now God's expression of life, love, and beauty to the world: "No-one has ever seen God; but if we love one another, God lives in us and His love is made complete in us" (1 John 4:12).

Labeled by the Vine

In addition to the year, every bottle of good wine is labeled with its name, that of the vine grower, and the strain of grape from which the wine was produced. As believers, we are all growing from the vine called Jesus. He has given us the Father's glory so that we can reveal this in our unity with each other (see John 17:22). The closer we draw to Him, submitting to His Holy Spirit, the more we see and reflect His glory and love. Our petty differences should not dim our corporate reflection of the beauty of Jesus.

Like the vineyard that produces the wine, our relationship with the Lord and with one another is moderated by the denomination, church, or country in which we have grown. But we do not develop and mature in the Christian faith by hiding ourselves under protective shelters of isolation and doctrine. We have to be exposed to the winds of change, the rain in its season, and the Sun of Righteousness (see Mal. 4:2). *We do not grow with theory and pattern, but by what feeds and empowers our lives,* and we can only bear fruit if we remain together as part of the True Vine.

Pruned to Remain Fruitful

Toward the end of each year, as the frost hardens the ground, the grower chops back the branches to ensure that the following season the vine will again produce large, succulent grapes. Jesus says that God the Father is the Gardener, and He continually prunes the branches on the vine to ensure their fruitfulness (see John 15:2). As unpruned branches, we start growing long and thin, heading in wrong directions and filling our minds and lives with distractions. We need regular challenges and reminders of the Truth to cut us back closer to the Vine. This is a major reason for writing this book—so that you, the reader, will be challenged by the Holy Spirit to think about your relationship with the Lord Jesus and with those who love and serve Him. Have we been growing so long in one direction, uncut and untended, that our lives bear little distinction from those of unbelievers? Or have we isolated ourselves from believers of other persuasions without noticing that we have grown away from the True Vine? I pray that you will be ready for the Divine Gardener to do a little pruning!

THE BEST WINE IS A COMPLEX MIX OF FLAVORS

Quite apart from the different bottles and labels, the color, taste, and texture of a wine can be remarkably varied. New wines are usually light and stimulate the palate. They are created fresh each year and provide the basis for many of the good wines that will develop over the succeeding years. Good, mature wines, in contrast, have depth or body and an exquisite mixture of subtle flavors that can be distinguished by the experienced palate. This depth and spectrum of flavors arises from the country of origin, the species of grape, the type of soil and local geology, the pressing and barreling process, and the time allowed for maturing.

Increasing the Character of the Wine

God is drawing us "from every tribe and language and people and nation" (Rev. 5:9). The variety is God's deliberate ploy to ensure that the Body has depth, is tasty, flavorful, and mature. The soil from which grapes grow can vary markedly—some good, some more rocky—and the degree to which the Word of God is received and accepted can affect the richness of the spiritual harvest (see Matt. 13:20-23). Wines grown in poor soil are most susceptible to breakdown. So our constant feeding from a good local church is important.

Following the wine analogy, it seems reasonable to have a wide variety of shades and types of Christian institutions and denominations, a church for every taste! But the components of individual churches are often limited, with roots in bitterness and rancor (see Heb. 12:15), grown in poor, dogmatic soil and not enriched by the complex flavors of diversity. Rather than multiplying by healthy growth, the number of churches in a city has often increased as a result of division. It may be good to have a wide choice, but if the quality is poor, is it worth tasting? By cutting ourselves off from other Christians with divergent traditions or opinions we become introspective, monochromatic, and tasteless. For any type of food or drink this is the last thing we want. Jesus said,

> *You are the salt of the earth. But if the salt loses its saltiness, how can it be made salty again? It is no longer good for anything, except to be thrown out and trampled by men* (Matthew 5:13).

Why should a non-Christian want to know what we as Christians believe if all they hear is our criticism of those with whom we fail to see eye to eye? Ask any believer what influenced him or her to trust in Christ, and in 99 percent of the cases the answer will be something like, "It was the loving character and caring nature of my friend." Unbelievers are not going to be convinced by our doctrine, but will be challenged by our lives. The Lord wants "to give drink to My people" full of aroma, tasty, and satisfying, "that they may proclaim My praise" (Isa. 43:18-21). Is your church a place where your friends or colleagues would want to be? How about getting together with some other churches for a day out hiking or even a wine-tasting? I guarantee you will get several of your unbelieving friends to join in.

WINE GAINS ITS FLAVOR IN THE FLASK

Winemaking is a science. The basic chemical reaction is the conversion of the natural sugars in the grapes into ethanol. The wine is generated in a container under carefully controlled conditions. Jesus used this process to pass comment on the attitudes of the Pharisees who had been confronting Him. He said,

> *No-one pours new wine into old wineskins. If he does, the new wine will burst the skins, the wine will run out and the wineskins will be ruined. No, new wine must be poured into new wineskins* (Luke 5:37-38).

New wine was something to enjoy and lift the spirits. It was to be the "treasure" to be contained in human "jars of clay" (see 2 Cor. 4:7), and it would be the evidence of the presence of God filling His new temple, the corporate Body of Christ (see Eph. 2:21). This spiritual wine would be detectable by the human senses, the tangible expression of the creative activity of the Holy Spirit in the new Church that was to be established. And this fresh new wine of the Spirit could not be contained by old religious "wineskins."

Jesus was not announcing a sudden reversal of God's Word. He said He had not come to abolish the Law or the Prophets, but to fulfill them (see Matt. 5:17). God's spiritual principles always remain the same, but the way they were to be applied was going change radically. Luke tells us that the old wineskins Jesus was addressing were the established structures and ordinances of the Mosaic Law, as interpreted, embellished, and applied by the legalistic Pharisees. But He was also referring to the restrictive mindset that was not able to contemplate a spiritual renewal with its new ways of doing things. It was the encrusted, human modifications of the original principles established by God that needed renewing.

Old Split Wineskins

In ancient Israel, new wine was poured into new wineskins to mature and to avoid breakdown of the alcohol (see Jer. 48:11). The wineskins—tanned skins of goats or sheep, turned inside out with the openings tied off—were tightly sealed with pitch.[1] As it dries out, leather cracks and splits easily. If such old cracked and brittle wineskins were used for the new, still-fermenting wine, the gas produced would stretch the skins, potentially causing splits and spillage of the wine.

The Mosaic and Pharisaic laws and traditions with their rigid limitations could not be stretched to accommodate the message that Jesus was bringing. The regular sacrifices of animals would not be necessary because Jesus would offer Himself as the ultimate sacrifice once and for all (see Heb. 9:12-14). The temple ceremonies would no longer be needed because each individual believer would become the temple of the Holy Spirit (see 1 Cor. 3:16). The laws about behavior would no longer need strict enforcement because they would be written in the believers' hearts by the Holy Spirit (see Heb. 8:10; Rom. 10:8).

Over the 2,000 years since Jesus spoke these words—particularly in the Western Church—well-meaning theologians and teachers have introduced interpretations and practical applications of the New Testament teaching on church structure. Mostly, this has been to make the teaching relevant to the times in which they lived. But while the times have changed, succeeding generations have held onto the structures without questioning their immediate relevance. Their inflexibility has tended to divide the Church rather than to unite us. As a result, God has seen fit to bring renewal and reformation to revitalize the Church and return believers to the vitality of a relationship with the living Lord Jesus.

Do rituals established hundreds of years ago still have meaning today? Should we still continue to inhabit organizational structures established in the wake of a previous powerful wave of the Holy Spirit? Are not these the old cracked wineskins that have lost their newness and flexibility? Do they even contain any of the old wine, or has it simply leaked out? To answer Jesus' prayer that we should be one (see John 17:21), we have to ask the Lord for new directions. Jesus says that it will not do to try and patch up the old system. In any case, the old wine stored in the cellar eventually runs dry. We cannot go on living indefinitely from the blessings of the past. The only sensible alternative is to provide new containers for the new wine.

Reassessing the Status Quo

When I was a boy, my father decided to support a small struggling church in our hometown for many decades spoken about in evangelical Christian circles as the "graveyard of evangelists." The church (led by lay elders rather than a full-time pastor) was presided over by an elderly man who, in his time, together with his wife, had held several positions in local government. Sadly, their behavior in these public offices had not endeared them to the local people. Their insistence, over many decades, on unaltered church services, equipped with fading old hymnbooks and uncomfortable wooden benches, in a dark nineteenth-century building with an uninviting, fenced gateway, did little to encourage the locals to enter this forbidding domain! When our family of five arrived, we immediately doubled the attendance figures. The regular Sunday evening sermon—"preaching the Gospel"—always seemed to me to be totally out of place, as there were almost never any unbelievers present! The wineskin was decidedly old and split. (This is the church I described in Chapter 3, now flourishing as a result of opening up to change, renovating the building, and working with other churches in the town).

At the end of His parable in Luke 5:39, Jesus makes an apparent throw-away comment: "No one after drinking old wine wants the new, for he says, 'The old is better.'" This can be translated, "It was so much better in the old days." Many churches and fellowships still have a hankering after the old days. Fear of failure, lack of trust in God, or simply nostalgia and unwillingness to change, lead us to confuse form and substance. We often retain a form of godliness, but deny its power (see 2 Tim. 3:5).

It is not just a matter of the hymnbooks we use, the order or timing of services we follow, the way in which leaders are elected, or the definition of the role of a minister. I am talking about our whole definition of "church" and how we "do" church. If we are to seek greater unity with each other on the basis of the blood of Jesus and to bring His peace and love to the modern world, we must find new ways to do this. We need flexible, extensible wineskins. We do not necessarily have to invalidate past approaches, but build on them and expand them. We must build bridges between churches and get out into the marketplace and homes.

Floyd McClung eloquently lays the groundwork for this reconstruction work:

> The Spirit [is] calling us to live the gospel within our culture rather than perpetuate church institutions that exist apart from our culture...It is time to bypass outdated institutions that occupy people with irrelevant focus...The Holy Spirit yearns to make Jesus real and known in our world...No one model will reach the whole world....The Spirit of God calls each generation to reimagine church for its own context and culture...God invites us to partner him and his mission by creating new wineskins.[2]

New, Flexible Containers

One of the ways that has proved widely successful in bringing together Christians of different backgrounds and persuasions is to hold concerts with Christian musicians. But there are less expensive or less highly-organized settings. A number of international Christian business associations organize dinners or breakfasts in hotels and invite speakers. We have also held a simple breakfast in a local restaurant on a Sunday morning to get English-speaking, international Christians and their friends together. Such simple events can be tremendous catalysts for enhancing contacts, breaking down barriers and misconceptions, and increasing our unity. What is relevant to your culture and environment?

The size, form, structure, and personnel of a Christian community in Scandinavia may differ considerably from that in Costa Rica or Indonesia. It should not be a question of "one size fits all." The Church should be all things to all people so that by all possible means we can win some (see 1 Cor. 9:22). The place to offer the "new wine" to the spiritual thirsty may be a café or a restaurant, a prison or a hospital, a barn or a cathedral, a discussion group or a liturgical service. It is not what we do or the way we do it that moves God's heart, but the reason why we do it! Jesus said that "where two or three come together in My name, there am I with them" (Matt. 18:20). Is not this also, in microcosm, an expression of church?

In his letters, Paul sometimes gives instructions about church order (see 1 Cor. 11; 14; 1 Tim. 2; 3). It is essential to recognize that these are not prescriptive instructions, but principles to be followed. I believe, at a time when formal religious meetings are losing their relevance, we should be taking the Word of Life to the people—into cafés, offices, factories, and the homes of those who would never consider setting foot in a church. Many people have become disillusioned with established churches. In Croatia, with its hot summers, life is spent on the streets and in the cafés. This is where we as Christians need to go *together* to show the love of Christ to those who do not know Him.

We do not all have to do everything the same way. People differ in their tastes, their preferences, emotional attachments, ways of working, abilities, social skills, enjoyment of exercise, singing, dancing, and talking. This diversity is not just found in a single local fellowship. One church may cater to those who prefer a regular liturgy, while others attract students and young people; another may have a ministry to business people. Why can we not embrace these various focuses and create new opportunities for the whole Body of believers? Renewing our wineskins means replacing the old with new elastic containers that can accommodate greater diversity.

In several areas of London, England, leaders of a variety of churches are beginning to meet regularly for prayer, joint services, and community outreach. In Lewisham, for instance, the churches collaborate in providing seminars on well-being—physical, mental, and spiritual. But this sort of initiative does not just have to come from church leaders. Most of them are full-time and have relatively little knowledge of the working environment. How about asking the believers in your workplace what you can do together? How can local government policies can be challenged, or can several churches coordinate work with students? We do not have to wait for the overworked pastor to come up with the proposal!

MATURING

By laying down the bottled wine, the fresh, astringent tannins, characteristic of a young wine, start to oxidize and become less sharp. The maturing wine begins to mellow and gains "body." This needs time, careful maintenance, and long-term, controlled storage. The Church also grows and matures as we spend time together, supporting and caring for one another. Different opinions and approaches, characteristics and temperaments are needed to form the Body.

Blending and Marrying Together

Wine, as used by Jesus in Luke 5, can be seen as the expression of the work of the Holy Spirit in both the individual and corporate lives of believing Christians. Our openness to His activity therefore determines the depth of our spiritual maturity. We "are being transformed into His likeness with ever-increasing glory, which comes from the Lord, who is the Spirit" (2 Cor. 3:18). The more time we spend in caring relationships with the Lord and with one another, the more "rounded" becomes our flavor, the more agreeable the "bouquet," and the more pleasant our "taste" to those around us. We need one another to rub off the rough edges of our lives, to blend together, to be effective in changing the lives of those who have never tasted that the Lord is good (see 1 Pet. 2:3).

As the fruity characteristics of the maturing wine begin to join together and complement each other, they are said to "marry" to provide the rounded taste of a good wine. Paul uses the same description of the relationship between a husband and wife to illustrate the Church (see Eph. 5). He points out that as we, the Bride of Christ, mature in our love for the Lord Jesus, so should a husband and wife deepen their love and care for one another.

Living in Germany in the 1980s, we were privileged to be able to provide hospitality for several days to Rev. Wilson G. Estes and his wife, Virginia, founders of Bethel Temple Christian Center in Abilene, Texas. At the time, both were well into their seventies. Their love for the Lord was deeply engrained in their relationship with one another. Wilson was attentive and concerned about his wife in a very natural and relaxed way. Virginia, for her part, made every attempt to please her husband. Even in her advanced years, she still took time each morning to look attractive. Without excess or show, it was very clear that this couple loved each other as deeply as they loved their Lord. They made a strong and lasting impression on both Elaine and me. Their example is one which we still seek to follow, not only in our marriage relationship, but also in our desire for the members of the Church to be "married" together in love for one another and for the Lord.

A marriage will never function if the partners keep asserting their differences. Love grows as we pursue the things that draw us together. Have you ever stopped to consider how much the Roman Catholic, Orthodox, Anglican, or Baptist colleague at work may have in common with you? Getting to know them will help, at least, bring our own understanding into perspective (see Prov. 27:17) and strengthen the collective spiritual impact on the local community.

Adding to the Flavor

Ulf Ekman, pastor and founder of Word of Life Ministries, Sweden, was quoted recently in an interview entitled, "Unity, the Key to Revival":

> You also need to be prepared to change and alter your attitude toward other Christians....The further we are from one another, the more simplified the perception we might have of the other....we are to relate to all the historical denominations, we can't simply skip the Catholics....it's important that we have a healthy understanding of the body of Christ.[3]

It is not our responsibility to decide who should be a member of the Body of Christ. If God has chosen someone or a group of people to add flavor to the mix, then we should integrate, not isolate them.[4] We are charged to accept the poor and the rich, the weak and the strong, slaves and the free, men and women, whether they agree with us, act like us, or share our opinions (see Rom. 14:1–15:7; James 2:1-13). Paul writes, "It is God who works in you to will and to act according to His good purpose" (Phil. 2:13), and His good purpose involves mixing our diversity together, inside and outside the church building, to create the final flavor.

I am not saying that we should simply jettison everything our churches or denominations have stood for over the years. To the contrary, "Do not move an ancient boundary stone set up by your forefathers" (Prov. 22:28). There are clear boundary stones for our faith which are vital to the spiritual integrity of the whole Church: the divinely inspired nature of the Bible and the doctrine of the triune God; the basis of salvation by faith in our redemption through the death of Christ and our justification by His resurrection; the sacraments of communion, baptism, and the sanctity of marriage. These boundary stones cannot be modified to fit the politically correct attitudes of the society we live in. But they can be retained while we increase our borders to take new land for the Kingdom of Heaven.

Pioneers are people who turn their backs on the comforts and familiarity of the past and push back the borders and boundaries. Pioneers of history brought variety into our Western kitchens—chocolate from South America, tea from the East, wine from Australia and South Africa. How can we enrich the "taste" of our local Christian community? Are we ready to take bold steps, even letting the Lord break off some branches and graft them into different vines (see Rom. 11:17-24)? This may mean that we can overcome some of the divisions of the past and start combining activities between previously antagonistic church groups.

WINE IS TO BE ENJOYED

At the wedding in Cana, Jesus was asked by His mother to help the host, because the wine had run out (see John 2:1-11). Jesus asked the servants to fill up some jars with water, which He then miraculously turned to wine. This was not just any old table wine. This was Grand Cru, the absolute best, which drew the wedding host's attention.

God only gives us the best. Jesus said, "I have come that they may have life, and have it to the full" (John 10:10)—not just in eternity, but here and now! He wants us to enjoy life with Him and with each other. He wants our joy to be "complete and overflowing" (John 15:11 AMP). Drawing an analogy with the effects of wine, Paul says, "Do not get drunk on wine…Instead, be [being] filled with the Spirit….Sing and make music in your heart to the Lord" (Eph. 5:18-19). This is a continuous process of renewal, the Holy Spirit changing us to be more like Christ as we pour out our lives in worship and service to God (see 2 Cor. 3:18). Good wine should not be kept in the cellar to turn bad, but poured out to be drunk and enjoyed. What better way of enjoying the wine of the Spirit by living, working, and praising God together. Our joy will be attractive—to our neighbors, our colleagues at work, and to our fellow Christians—every day.

In Psalm 133:1, David says that it is "good and pleasant…when brothers live together in unity." The complex components of a good wine give it a fragrant bouquet and a smooth, lingering, delicious taste. When Christians live together in unity, encouraging one another to do good, we become "the fragrance of the knowledge of Him…the aroma of Christ among those who are being saved" (2 Cor. 2:14-15). We also get blessed ourselves! Not only can we be of practical help to one another, we can complement each other's capabilities in reaching out to the community. I am always encouraged when I hear from other Christians about what God is doing outside my immediate circle of influence. I am uplifted by praising God in interdenominational services. And you can never tell when you may need to call on the help of the new Christian friend you have made. It is indeed good and pleasant to be united together with others who share our love for the Lord.

ENDNOTES

1. http://www.bible-history.com/isbe/W/WINE%3B+WINE+PRESS/.

2. Floyd McClung, *You See Bones, I See an Army* (Eastbourne, UK: David C. Cook, 2007), 40, 42.

3. *Word of Life Missions Magazine*, No. 4, 2007.

4. The exception to this injunction is when a leader may need to lovingly admonish a member of his church who is clearly acting in a way that is harmful either to himself or to others in the fellowship, as outlined in Second Timothy 2:25-26.

CHAPTER 9

THE LIGHT OF THE WORLD

PEOPLE ARE LIKE STAINED-GLASS WINDOWS.
THEY SPARKLE AND SHINE WHEN THE SUN IS OUT,
BUT WHEN THE DARKNESS SETS IN THEIR TRUE BEAUTY
IS REVEALED ONLY IF THERE IS A LIGHT FROM WITHIN.

—Elisabeth Kübler-Ross,
Swiss-American psychiatrist
and author, 1926–2004

A unique feature of the old part of Zagreb is that several of the narrow streets are still lit by gas. A spectacle for tourists, the lights are ignited each evening and extinguished each morning by attendant gas lighters. Introduced in the late nineteenth century, the gaslights must have been welcome to the citizens who had been stumbling around the dark cobbled streets by the light of lanterns. Cities these days rely on bright electric lighting. We take it for granted that we can walk along a well-lit street at night without any difficulty.

Jesus said to His disciples, "You are the light of the world....let your light shine before men, that they may see your good deeds and praise your Father in heaven" (Matt. 5:14,16). In a world darkened

141

by the enemy, Christians should be shining brightly, providing clarity and understanding to those in our vicinity to the praise of God (see 1 Pet. 2:12). For this, we require the Holy Spirit's power, which is released when we live and act in unity (see Ps. 133:1-3; Eph. 3:20), enabling our good deeds to have an impact on the world. But if our light is so dim that nobody can distinguish anything, how can this be to the praise of God?

BRIGHT, SHINING LIGHTS

Many churches are just following the traditions of a previous era of spiritual blessing, and their light has grown dim, like the old gas lamps. Sadly, we adjust to the weak spiritual light, as though revival were a thing of the past. But God has not changed. We do not need a new Holy Spirit, a modern, environmentally friendly source of spiritual energy. If we are drawing on the wrong sources, based on our own ideas and strength, like the gas lamp attendants, we are actively "putting out the Spirit's fire" (see 1 Thess. 5:19).

Short-Circuiting the Power Supply

Paul, in the section on unity, warns the Ephesian believers not to "grieve the Holy Spirit of God" when talking to each other (Eph. 4:30). Commenting on this verse, Francis Foulkes explains that "the Spirit is the bond of the life of fellowship, and the sin of offending a brother by false word or act especially grieves him."[1] Each of us is responsible for maintaining our personal relationship with the Lord, remaining open to His Holy Spirit. But as members of Christ's Body, the interrelational sins we considered in Chapter 6 can block the power supply.

By cheating our fellow believers, criticizing them, telling lies, or slandering one another, we grieve the Holy Spirit within us, our unity is damaged, our power supply is cut, God is robbed of praise, and we reduce our impact on the world around us. A disunited church is one in which the power supply is dissipated, the lines of supply are short-circuited, the batteries are no longer being charged properly, and the light beam is unfocused. We become dim, flickering lamps, unnoticeable among the distracting, gaudy red-light districts of the societies we live in. Who wants a light that barely functions? We should definitely avoid arguments about the "theological" lamp another believer is using. It is likely that both his light and mine will go out!

Besides, in many situations, it is not the size or shape of the lamp that counts, but whether the power is flowing through it: "You will receive power when the Holy Spirit comes on you; and you will be My witnesses" (Acts 1:8). The brightness of our light is dependent on the extent to which *together* we are allowing the Holy Spirit to work through us. Do you and I make a difference to the world around us? By living in unity with fellow believers, are we revealing a lifestyle which is different and attractive?

Increasing the Light Intensity

As individuals and in our relationships with other Christians, our spiritual light should be burning brighter and brighter for Christ's glory (see 2 Cor. 3:18). The halo of light should be increasing in intensity and circumference so that more of the people around us are bathed in the glow. This is what Daniel prophesied, that "those who are wise will shine like the brightness of the heavens, and those who lead many to righteousness, like the stars for ever and ever" (Dan. 12:3). This is the destiny of the Church—to burn increasingly brighter so that many may be led to righteousness and salvation!

Around the world you will find megachurches with thousands of members, impacting their cities and the nation. Willow Creek Community Church in the U.S., pastored by Bill Hybels, is a good example. These churches have not grown by keeping themselves aloof from other streams of Christianity. To the contrary! Willow Creek and many other large churches are characterized by their work with a variety of Christian groups—training pastors, business leaders, and others from all backgrounds and walks of life. They are exerting a strong impact on society because their light is shining into the streets and backyards of very diverse groups of believers and unbelievers alike.

In order to impact our cities and nations, we must coordinate our activities and be accountable to one another. A single light bulb can only generate a limited light intensity. The most powerful floodlights consist of a battery of lights, and a large hall is effectively lit by many lamps. The task facing the Church today is far greater than any one group of Christians can achieve alone. We have to shine together.

Power With a Purpose

The Bible tells us that when the Holy Spirit came upon men and women, the result was often dramatic and always brought honor and glory to God. Deborah, the leader of Israel during the time of the judges, acknowledged that the combined effect of the willing commitment of the people and the power of the Lord was responsible for the total defeat of the Canaanite army that they were celebrating (see Judg. 5:2,4).

Young Saul was astounded at the fear of the citizens of the city of Jabesh Gilead which was under siege by the Ammonites. The power of the Spirit of God who came upon him proved so convincing that 333,000 soldiers turned out "as one man" to totally destroy the enemy army (1 Sam. 11:6-8).

At Pentecost, the presence of the Holy Spirit was evidenced by tongues of flame, praise to God in different languages, and the powerful preaching of Peter (see Acts 2). Today, as well, things happen when we willingly allow the Holy Spirit the freedom to work in our lives—unexpected events, unimaginable victories. This is power with a purpose!

But being spiritually powerful does not just mean preaching the Gospel. This is only one aspect of the healthy functioning of the Body of Christ. Our daily lives should first gain the respect of people around us so that they will be willing to listen. *Light is effective not because it burns, but because it is there.* Salt is effective because of its presence. In the long run, our availability and willingness to help people is more effective than just warning them to be saved! "Live such good lives among the pagans that, though they accuse you of doing wrong, they may see your good deeds and glorify God on the day He visits us" (1 Pet. 2:12). A Spirit-filled, powerful, united Church will inevitably differ visibly from and have an influence on the society around it. Our practical contribution to the needs of the community, particularly for members of the family of believers (see Gal. 6:10), should be the natural outworking of the Holy Spirit in us as a united Church. This is practical love at work. In an economically and morally unstable society, the Church should be the beacon of stable light.

ONE IN HEART AND MIND

The presence and power of the Holy Spirit in the life of the Church, and the degree to which Christians are really united, are mutually inseparable. He was able to move with such dramatic power at Pentecost because the disciples had joined together in prayer (see Acts 1:14) and "were all together in one place" (Acts 2:1). His power is not just evidenced in signs, miracles, and conversions, but also in greater love among believers for one another and a desire to work together. There is only one Holy Spirit, and He is indivisible!

A Spirit-given concern for the health of the Body of Christ inevitably raises awareness of its various needs. Paul obviously understood something about physical health as he trained himself to bring his desires and habits into line with his ministry of evangelism (see 1 Cor. 9:27). But this is also true of the Body of Christ. Our task is to work and train for the Kingdom of God. We should care for each other's spiritual and physical welfare to be able to fulfill this calling.

This is where being of one mind and heart comes in. It is much easier to work together when we share a common goal. Jesus gave us the goal to "seek first [God's] Kingdom and His righteousness" (Matt. 6:33). Mutually shared concern and joint prayer for God's righteousness to be revealed in our governments, factories, and schools provide the motivation to follow a common direction. As a result of the churches in my hometown working together, not only have individual churches benefited, but many individual believers have been helped in unexpected ways. Musicians have formed groups, elderly women have received practical assistance, business people have been working together, and unbelievers are being saved. *The synergy of joint contributions is always greater than the sum of individual, uncoordinated activities.* The light of the Church becomes focused and shines much brighter.

WILLING TO SHARE

As a consequence of their oneness, the believers in the Jerusalem church "had everything in common" and "shared everything they had" (Acts 2:44; 4:32). The revelation of a single uniting purpose to glorify God and build His Kingdom automatically led to a selfless desire to share with others in the church, and the systems were soon put in place to do this.

Maintaining Communication and Support Systems

In the human body, the eye is not adjacent to, but still guides the foot, which in turn carries the eye. So in the Body of Christ we do not necessarily have to work, agree, or even pray *with* each other, but to work, agree, and pray *for* each other. Paul states that "each member belongs to all the others" (Rom. 12:5), so once incorporated into the Body, we need to pull our weight in contributing to its functions.

The nervous system for information, the blood system for nutrition, and the blood and lymph systems for defense are all needed for good health. Similarly, the parts of the Body of Christ need to be in contact to maintain good spiritual health: "If one part suffers, every part suffers with it" (1 Cor. 12:26). If I cut a finger, have a headache, or get something in my eye, then my whole body responds to the discomfort, every part working together to relieve the pain and remove the source of the problem. Human skin is supplied with a dense network of sensory nerves, which are activated by heat, changes in acidity, damaging chemicals, itch, injury, and pain. In the very rare condition of congenital insensitivity to pain, the fibers that mediate pain are absent from birth—patients often fail to notice that they have injured themselves. Early death is common.

In the spiritual sense, this seems to be the condition in several parts of the Church. There is little recognition or realization of the pain and injury arising in other parts of the Body because the "nerves," the lines of communication between us, are not functioning. *We are not aware of our mutual needs because we have no interest in sharing with each other!* This is not just the responsibility of the leaders of local churches. We should all be looking for ways to help those around us, particularly our fellow believers. A first step would be to make contact with the various Christian groups in your town.

Keep Things Moving

The gifts and possessions God gives us are intended to be of benefit to the Body of Christ. In the human body, nothing is static. What we eat and drink is absorbed from the gastrointestinal tract and distributed via the blood to every organ and cell in the body. The energy released from cell metabolism keeps our hearts pumping, our muscles working, our organs functioning, and our defenses strong. If a blood vessel gets blocked, the circulation is interrupted, local nutrition blocked, waste products accumulate, and function is compromised. How many clots and thromboses are we currently accepting in the Church? Chronic unmet needs in a church indicate that somewhere the circulation of practical love has been interrupted.

The "circulation" among the early Christians did not just involve money and possessions. They opened their homes for church meetings and for meals (see Acts 2:46). Paul too encouraged the Roman believers to "share with God's people who are in need. Practise hospitality" (Rom. 12:13). He tells the Christians in Galatia not just to expect their leaders to do all the teaching and work— those who are taught should share good things with the instructor as well (see Gal. 6:6). It was not, is not, nor ever will be a question of what we have or do not have, but what we *do* with our time, abilities, and possessions!

MEETING ALL NEEDS

An immediate result of the coming of the Holy Spirit at Pentecost was that the Christians sold "their possessions and goods, [and] gave to anyone as he had need" (Acts 2:45). Widows were among the most in need because they had no one to provide for them (see Acts 6:1). Giving to them was not just a flash-in-the-pan response. It was seen by the leaders, such as James, as an essential aspect of the lifestyle God expects (see James 1:27). Even in the early church, though, providing for needs was not always done with the best of motives, as the Hebrew widows were getting preferential treatment over the Greek widows (see Acts 6:1). This highlights the fact that our giving should be a natural response to the guidance of the Holy Spirit, not based on our subjective assessment of the "worth" of the potential recipient. Obviously, we have to be "good stewards" of the gifts and possessions we have each received through God's grace (see 1 Pet. 4:10 KJV), and we cannot provide, individually, for all needs. But if our fundamental attitude is one of generosity, we are inevitably more sensitive to motivation by the Holy Spirit when we are confronted with a specific need we are able to meet. This is especially true when we can each contribute toward the corporate provision for a need within the Church.

A Lifestyle of Giving

Generosity is a crucial aspect of "letting our light shine," revealing our practical approach to others' needs. *Our faith is shown by what we do (see James 2:18), not by the gifts or ministries we claim to have received from the Holy Spirit!*

Within a short space of time, among the thousands of new Christians in Jerusalem, all needs were being met (see Acts 4:34). Initially, this provision was the personal priority of the church leaders (see Acts 4:35). Later, deacons were appointed for the task (see Acts 6:3-4). We also have our roles to play. We do not have to wait to be told; we only have to open our eyes and help those in front of our noses. To some, like my wife Elaine, this comes naturally. If you are like me, you must let the Holy Spirit soften your heart.

The needs in the early church included preparing and distributing food, giving money, providing accommodation, organizing church meetings, offering hospitality, and healing and caring for the sick; they were met as they arose (see Acts 4:34). Providing for needs is not a question of automatic giving into the collection every Sunday. It is a lifestyle. In a functioning citywide church, personal needs should be addressed wherever and whenever they arise. It would help if the needs were shared among churches. At least we can pray for each other.

God does not begrudge anyone an enjoyable life. We should expect reasonable remuneration for our daily work (see Luke 10:7), provide for our families and our dependents (see 1 Tim. 5:8), and use wisely the money we have received by God's grace (see Luke 19:23). I have found that dividing my salary each month into set percentages for living, saving, and giving is helpful. It is right to value the abilities, gifts, and possessions God has given us, but also to use them "so that the body of Christ may be built up" (Eph. 4:12). This is done most effectively in both the physical and spiritual worlds by good investment. In the parable of the talents, Jesus tells us to put our gifts to work in God's Kingdom because, by doing so, God is able to trust us with more (see Matt. 25:14-30). Giving to meet the needs of other believers is a much safer investment with a much greater return than anything Wall Street can offer!

Mutual Benefits

The principle involved here is reciprocity, as succinctly stated by Jesus Himself: "Give, and it will be given to you" (Luke 6:38). Our cheerful giving to others in response to God's love opens doors in the spiritual realm. The Jews were encouraged to give tithes so that God would open the doors of Heaven to bless them (see Mal. 3:10).

Jesus promises that we shall also receive a blessing—in some area of our lives—as a result of a generous lifestyle. As Paul says, if we earn well and give to meet others' needs, those same believers may provide for us when we ourselves are in need (see 2 Cor. 8:13-14). The benefits of giving are always mutual!

Just recently, a friend in another church (one to whom we had given financial support the previous year) found a handyman in a third church who came and fixed our plumbing. Not long ago, Elaine had done the ironing for this man's wife when she was pregnant with her seventh child! So we all ended up thanking the Lord. In such instances, doctrine and theology are irrelevant!

Paul compliments the poor churches in Macedonia for giving to the needs of other less-fortunate churches and admonishes the rich Corinthian church to do the same (see 2 Cor. 8; 9). Imagine the blessing that would result if believers from different churches shared their abilities and possessions with needy people in other churches in their own city, let alone in other countries! Why struggle to repair the television of the old lady from my church when there's a professional television repairman in the church down the road who can help? Or perhaps we do not even know he is there, because nobody from our church ever met him!

THE GOOD, THE NOT-SO-GOOD, AND THE INJURED

If the light of the Church is to shine brightly, then communication, care, and sharing first need to be put into practice at home, among our brothers and sisters in faith. But we are only going to impact the world around us if our light is being directed into the darkness. We have to take the Light of the World outside our church buildings.

Traveling south to Jerusalem, Jesus and His disciples passed through the province of Samaria. There, Jews had intermixed with people forcibly brought in by the Assyrians and Babylonians, and these Samaritans had modified Jewish traditions, believing Mount Gerazim to be their most holy place, not Mount Zion in Jerusalem.

Like many Christian denominations, differences in doctrine and tradition were grounds for the Jews and Samaritans to avoid each other. As a result, Jesus and His Jewish disciples were turned away from a Samaritan village (see Luke 9:51-56), and in the whole next section of Luke's narrative, Jesus talks about being hospitable. In the middle of this, a teacher of the law asks, "Who is my neighbor? To whom should I be kind and hospitable?" So Jesus tells the parable about a man traveling down the road from Jerusalem to Jericho (see Luke 10:25-37).

The Injured

The road from Jerusalem to Jericho passes through a dry, deserted area. Not a place to get into trouble! Perhaps the traveler Jesus referred to was a Jewish merchant taking goods to the bustling market in Jericho. On the way, he is robbed, beaten, and left half-dead (see Luke 10:30).

Many people we meet, also fellow believers, have been robbed by misfortune, beaten by circumstances, or injured by abuse. They are all around us, at work, in our neighborhood, among our families and friends—the single mother, the lonely business person, the anxious colleague. Among believers, quarreling, overzealous discipling, and the imposition of strict religious behavior leave behind wounded, hurting Christians. They become fearful, mistrusting, and weak. Can we recognize the injured people? In Jesus' parable, the man was "half-dead," no longer able to decide whether he wanted to be helped! Do we need to be half-dead before we accept help and advice from our brothers and sisters?

The Not-So-Good

The priest and the Levite were no use at all; they "passed by on the other side" (Luke 10:31-32). The priest's task was to shepherd the people, while the Levite cared for the house of God and taught. Like many Christians today, they were more concerned about their own position and doctrinal purity. They did not want to contaminate themselves with people in need.

Many of us are blessed with possessions, abilities, and a treasure trove of scriptural knowledge. We could help and counsel many others, including fellow believers, if we were willing to leave the confines of our safe local church environment for the community and workplace outside. There are "half-dead" people across our backyards, but perhaps we have never looked. *It is not in our "Christian club" that we shall find the neighbor to love, but out on the desolate, dangerous road to Jericho!*

The Good

Now along comes the Samaritan—a foreigner, with no national allegiance to any local traveler. Shunned by the Jews, he would not have been moved by religious conscience. Presumably a wealthy merchant, he would have felt no social pressure to assist someone less fortunate. And to Jesus' disciples, this man represented the very people who had recently refused them accommodation! In every way, he was a most unlikely source of help. But he sees his "neighbor" in need and unhesitatingly comes to the man's aid. Once again, it is not who we are, but what we *do* that counts!

The Samaritan did not ask the man's race, religion, or profession. He did not think, as Jesus' disciples might have, "this is one of those arrogant, heretical types who rejected me." He overlooked any potential differences and just saw the man's need. He got involved, used his expensive "vehicle" to carry the injured man, and paid for the man's care. He was a practical illustration of what Jesus had said earlier: "Love your enemies, do good to those who hate you" (Luke 6:27-36), especially if they belong to God's family. He set an example and encouraged others to help. He followed up and made sure the job was finished.

Street Pastors, in the United Kingdom, are following this example.[2] Christians of all denominations, trained for a few weeks and working with the police, community leaders, and local agencies, get to know people as they leave pubs, clubs, and discos, finding out their needs and how they can be helped. Started in 2002, to help stem the increasing tide of violent crime, there are now 100 teams of Street Pastors across the country. Crime rates in many areas have decreased, drawing the attention of national media. In the British parliament they have been presented as an illustration of Christian faith that is "alive and kicking." Is this something you can start doing in your neighborhood?

Finally, we come to the innkeeper—another good guy—who provided a room for the injured man and cared for him. The Samaritan could not do everything himself, and the innkeeper was also prepared to go beyond his duty (though he got paid for it!). How open is our home, our car, our church to the neighbor or fellow believer in need?

Not long ago, my son, who lives in Scotland, took a train into the mountains on his day off to pray. Although it was a Monday, he felt God was telling him to find a church in the village. The only church he found was locked. Taking the train to the next town, he found a couple of other churches—all locked. The lesson was clear. When it comes to showing practical concern for others, are we "only open on Sundays"?

> *"Which of these three do you think was a neighbour to the man who fell into the hands of robbers?" The expert in the law replied, "The one who had mercy on him." Jesus told him, "Go and do likewise"* (Luke 10:36-37).

ENDNOTES

1. Francis Foulkes, *The Epistle of Paul to the Ephesians. An Introduction and Commentary* (London, UK: Tyndale Press, 1963), 136.

2. http://www.streetpastors.co.uk/.

CHAPTER **10**

REACHING THE CITY

NOW, AS I SAID, THE WAY TO THE CELESTIAL CITY
LIES JUST THROUGH THIS TOWN,
WHERE THIS LUSTY FAIR IS KEPT;
AND HE THAT WILL GO TO THE CITY,
AND YET NOT GO THROUGH THIS TOWN,
MUST NEEDS GO OUT OF THE WORLD.

—John Bunyan, English clergyman, 1628–1688,
in *The Pilgrim's Progress*

The Church is called to be the Light of the world, not only of our local community. God is interested in the fate of individual cities and whole nations and whether they follow His standards of righteousness and justice (see Prov. 13:34; Isa. 51:4-5). During His ministry, Jesus expressed His concern for the populations of Jerusalem and the Galilean towns (see Matt. 23:37; Luke 10: 8-15).

Taking Isaiah's prophecy and applying it to Jesus, Matthew says, "He will proclaim justice to the nations…In His name the nations will put their hope" (Isa. 42:1-4; Matt. 12:18,21). Consequently, as Jesus' disciples, we have been commanded to "go and make disciples of all

155

nations" (Matt. 28:19). This is why we need a strong, united, loving, and outreaching Church, because the whole world is open to the light of God's truth as never before. For most of us, this means reaching our home country, the town where we grew up, or the city where we have found a job. For others, like me and my family, work may take us to other countries. But wherever God leads us, we can be used to bless other Christians, our colleagues, and neighbors as we "seek the peace and prosperity of the city to which [God] has carried [us]" (Jer. 29:7).

Imagine that for two hundred years your country has had a traditional enemy, a large, brutal neighboring nation that holds no regard for your beliefs. You do not feel particularly secure in the shadow of this potential threat, although there is currently an uneasy peace. Then God says, "Go and be a missionary to the capital of that nation!" How would you feel? Well, that's exactly how Jonah felt and how many of us feel about the world beyond our doorstep. "I have enough to do here. Besides, I do not like those people out there. Why should I be bothered? I have a comfortable lifestyle now, so please do not spoil it. Someone else is responsible for what happens elsewhere." I believe we can learn a great deal from Jonah's experience, as individual Christians and as the Church.

A REJECTED CALL

Jonah lived in Israel under Jeroboam II, not a God-fearing king, but one who restored Israel to some strength and stability. Jonah was an established, recognized prophet in this reasonably secure country (see 2 Kings 14:25), comfortable giving encouraging prophecies at home. Now God tells him to go and preach a condemnatory message against the city of Nineveh (see Jon. 1:2), whose 120,000 inhabitants possessed no knowledge of the God of Israel (see Jon. 3:3; 4:11). This was a bit too risky for Jonah. Besides, God had a habit of showing mercy, and Jonah had no desire to go and be "nice" to his enemies (see Jon. 4:2).

Taking Things Easy

Many of us Christians are afraid of leaving our comfortable, de-nominational nests and stepping out into unknown territory. We pamper our network of spiritually inbred friends and enjoy the solace of the familiar ecclesiastical rituals. Without a goal to work for, a purpose to pray over, or a message to talk about, we concentrate on making life comfortable, decorating the building, organizing entertaining events, and ignoring the command to "go." But is that where God really wants us to be?

Jonah wanted to stay with the Jewish people he was used to. Why go anywhere else? Yahweh was the exclusive God of Israel—or was He? Centuries earlier, God had promised Abraham that through him and his descendants all nations would be blessed (see Gen. 18:18; 22:18). So were the Jews being unnecessarily exclusive? Was God's message to Jonah an indicator that they should have been sharing God's blessing with others all along?

In our united work for God, we cannot all stay in the same place. A big church gets too comfortable and anonymous. God wants us out in the city, where it is tough and hard, where we might get shouted at and wounded, but where there are needy people to be reached. If we are going to allow our light to shine more brightly, then we have to invade the darkness—whether the darkness of a corrupt, greedy, and exploitative world or the darkness of unknown, unexplored territories. In maps of the world, prepared in the fourteenth or fifteenth centuries, unexplored regions would commonly be labeled, "Here there be dragons." And that would be a sufficient deterrent for many to venture anywhere near those parts. How many "dragons" do we imagine occupy areas we are afraid to enter?

Faith in Action

God responds to faith, not to fear or inactivity (see Rom. 14:23). So we experience His power when we add our faith to His Word and step out, expecting Him to act. After eighteen years in Germany, we had come to the conclusion that God wanted us to put down our roots there. We were elders in a strong Christian fellowship and had recently bought a house. The business I was running was not growing much, our role in the church was changing, and our two eldest children were about to leave the nest, so we did suspect that change was in the air.

Then the phone rang with the challenging offer of a job in Zagreb, Croatia, a country just emerging from a war that had ended two years earlier. Elaine was ready to pack up and go! I was more cautious. But on a business trip to Tokyo the Lord reminded me that "no one who has left home…will fail to receive a hundred times as much in this present age…and in the age to come, eternal life" (Mark 10:29-30). I knew we had to go to Zagreb and that God would take care of us—which He has done in many wonderful ways—but that is another book!

No matter how small the issue or how large the challenge, it is our faith in His Word, put into action in the expectation that God is going to respond, that releases His power to act in specific and sometimes miraculous ways. This applies to our individual lives, our church fellowship, and to our involvement with fellow believers across the city.

Do we really *expect* the Holy Spirit to work in power through united Christians in our locality? "Without faith it is impossible to please God" (Heb. 11:6). Has our faith been reduced to the repetition of a few familiar prayers or Bible verses and attendance at church services? Do you find yourself thinking, *How can I even entertain the idea of doing anything with other Christians when it is so hard just to keep going in my own church and job?*

Struggling to maintain the status quo, we fail to recognize that it is the Lord's battle, not ours. *It is not our life to live, but the life that He lives in us* (see Gal. 2:20). We *must* believe that He is the Lord who is there (*Jehovah-Shammah,* see Ezek. 48:35) and that He is waiting to reward our faith by giving us the power to implement His plan. If we have put our trust in Jesus, through the salvation He paid for with His blood, and have received the Holy Spirit by believing (see Gal. 3:2), we should now "live by the Spirit" (Gal. 5:16) with the same faith. And this means we have to leave our comfort zones.

Coordinated Action

To Jonah, God said, "Go to Nineveh." To us, Jesus says, "Go to *all* nations" (Matt. 28:19). He was proclaiming the vision of a powerful united Church, cooperating to reach every corner of our society. And as He was about to ascend, Jesus prophesied that "repentance and forgiveness of sins [would] be preached in His name to all nations, beginning at Jerusalem" (Luke 24:47). We are brought together in unity through repentance and forgiveness, and the same message is to be preached to bring others into God's Kingdom, beginning with the city where we live. To enable us to preach this message in unity, we are to be "clothed with power from on high" (Luke 24:49). The Holy Spirit may not send us to another country, but He will certainly send us beyond the boundaries of our preconceptions, aversions, fears, and personal preferences. Unlike Jonah, God does not expect us to work on our own, but to connect with other Christian fellowships—to complement, not compete with one another in our outreach.

THE RECALCITRANT COURIER

Jonah, assuming that God would find other ways of challenging him if he stayed in Israel, ran in the opposite direction, away from Nineveh. He headed for Tarshish, thought to have been a port on the coast of Spain, but certainly far away from Israel and Nineveh.

No Place to Hide

If we fail to respond to God's call, even by doing nothing, *we cannot expect to get away with our disobedience!* The enemy will find a way to occupy us! As individuals, time is often stolen with such distractions as excessive television watching. As churches ignoring the Divine Commission to reach out into the community, we see all the problems in one another and soon start tearing each other apart.

On the other hand, when God calls, there is no place to hide (see Ps. 139:7). Adam hid in the bushes till God found him (see Gen. 3:8-9). Jacob ran away from home to escape from his brother Esau, and God confronted him in a dream at Bethel (see Gen. 28:11-19).

Moses killed a soldier and fled from Egypt into the desert where God caught up with him by speaking from the burning bush (see Exod. 3:1-2). Saul pathetically and pointlessly tried to hide behind some baggage when he was to be anointed king of Israel (see 1 Sam. 10:22). When Israel collectively abandoned her calling to serve God, He sent prophets to warn the people and finally had the nation exiled to bring them to their senses. God is too concerned about the eternal fate of His family to allow us to wander off on our own and not chase after us.

Many churches develop the "ostrich syndrome," burying their heads in the sand: "Perhaps if we keep our heads down and just take care of ourselves no one will notice." If we deliberately avoid contacts with believers in other fellowships, what chance do we have of winning the interest of people who have no time for God? There is little likelihood of spiritual growth or revival if we turn in on ourselves in denial of His call.

Jonah boarded a ship for Tarshish, which sailed straight into a violent storm that threatened to destroy the whole ship's company. He ended up being thrown into the sea (see Jon. 1:4-16). God's call is irrevocable (see Rom. 11:29). So if we are not flowing with His plan, then we are working against Him. *Uniting with other Christians to reach our communities is the command of Jesus, His continual prayer, and the goal of His ministry on earth.*

We have already seen that disunity brings sickness and death (see 1 Cor. 11:29-30). How many of the storms we experience in our families, work, or churches have we brought on ourselves through our stubborn rejection of Christ's prayer for the unity of His people (see John 17:23)? When Jesus appeared to Paul on his way to Damascus to take more Christians prisoner, He gave a precise analysis of the shocked Pharisee's mental state: "It is hard for you to kick against the goads" (Acts 26:14). "It makes your life a misery to resist God's gentle prodding." Paul had to admit his tragic error and capitulate to his Savior. What are we running away from? It is time to face up to the fact that living and working together in unity is where God "bestows His blessing" (Ps. 133:3).

At the End of Our Tether

Just when everything seemed to be lost—including his own life—Jonah, through God's extraordinary mercy, was given one last chance to sort out his priorities. He spent three days thinking about it in the dark, smelly belly of a fish! Finally, he vowed to make good what he had so miserably failed to do up till then (see Jon. 2:9).

God has frequently allowed difficulties to build up in my life to the point where I think they are insurmountable. Only then does He unexpectedly provide the solution. This has happened so often I have come to believe that waiting for me to give up is His systematic method of extending my faith. It may be in my professional life, when the poor economic and financial prospects seem unending and employment appears a distant dream. Then again, the opportunities for our children's education may just seem to be getting worse. In the local church, the members may be voting with their feet and there does not seem to be anywhere else to go. It is then that God provides the answers to our prayers. God brings us to the end of our own capabilities to show that He is the greatest! Then He can tell us what He has been waiting to say all the time!

What is the Lord asking of you and me? How often does He have to repeat His message? In our cities, many need the mercy and love of God. They will not be reached by a few isolated groups of downcast believers, hoping that God will perform a miracle of multiple salvations. Nor are corruption and moral and economic decline going to be reversed by each denomination holding its own little conference. A big challenge requires a big solution! And God has already provided this—the Church living in unity and reaching out in love together in the power of the Holy Spirit. Whatever your city's challenge, the answer is the same!

A REPENTANT CITY

Back out of the mess he had got himself into, Jonah again receives God's orders: "Go to the great city of Nineveh and proclaim the message I give you" (Jon. 3:2). Nineveh was the largest city in the known world at the time, and God was concerned about its citizens. According to United Nations figures, in Europe at the turn of the millennium over 70 percent of the population was living in urban areas, and in North America nearly 80 percent. In the world's most highly populated country, China, the figure was around 35 percent in 2000 and was expected to nearly double over the succeeding 25 years.[1] The same is true of most of the African continent. The task God gave to Jonah has never been more up-to-date than in the twenty-first century!

The City Is Where Things Happen

Henry Drummond, a nineteenth-century Scottish evangelist and scientist who challenged Christians of his day to make their faith practical, said in an address in 1893,

> To make good cities—that is for the present hour the main work of Christianity. For the city is strategic…
> What Christianity waits for also, as its final apologetic and justification to the world, is the founding of a city which shall be in visible reality a city of God.[2]

This is also what God says, "Seek the peace and prosperity of the city to which I have carried you…Pray to the Lord for it, because if it prospers, you too will prosper" (Jer. 29:7). It is the huge, anonymous, diverse, bustling cities that are the mission field for the Church today. But the message we have been given to preach has not changed for the past 2,000 years. "The gospel is the power of God for the salvation of everyone who believes" (see Rom. 1:16). It is just that we need a Holy Spirit-empowered, united Church to reach those cities.

The modern metropolis is much bigger and more complex than the agriculture-driven hubs of the Ancient World. Modern cities have a variety of layers. Culture is often divided among city center concert halls, theatres, and museums; inner city ethnic neighborhoods; and suburban housing communities. Each may have their own character and local color. The economic centers are frequently the business, banking, and trading districts. Social networks, public transport, and other forms of communication may be well distributed, but also vary in quality and density, commonly distributed around local hubs. In other words, modern cities have multiple centers, in effect, being conurbations of different villages. Unless people are integrated into social groups, it is easy to be alone in a big city. A divided and dislocated church is not very effective in reaching the city's inhabitants (see Matt. 12:25). To reach into all its dark corners, a diversity of gifts among whole communities and churches are needed, with varieties of ministries. Some may be directed toward students, others toward the business community, still others to the down-and-outs of society.

In London and several other cities around the world, churches are forming networks, each following their own particular focus but in a coordinated, cooperative, and prayerful manner. In this sort of environment, we can train all members, encouraging them to devise new ways to impact their workplaces and neighborhoods. Older members with years of professional experience can be valuable practical advisors to church leaders.

Lack of Enthusiasm

Finally, Jonah went to Nineveh, with the message that disaster was going to strike the city within forty days (see Jon. 3:4). We are not told whether his message contained any recommendation to repent. Not knowing the God of Israel, why should the inhabitants take any notice of what Jonah said? From subsequent events, it seems that Jonah really wanted the city to collapse in fire and ashes. This was how God dealt with the rest of Israel's wicked enemies, so why not Nineveh as well?

Jonah's attitude was not much different from that of many of us. We are quick to condemn the government or local city council for their mistakes and incompetence. We find fault with our church leaders and accuse fellow Christians in other churches of doctrinal error. We question people's motives for doing good, complain about their wrong use of our money, and are happy when they get what is coming to them. For many years, I joined other European friends in castigating U.S. government policy, painting the U.S. as an arrogant, all-consuming nation—until the Lord made it clear that this was not the attitude that I as a member of His family should take. These days, I am a lot more circumspect with my comments and seek to be encouraging rather than condemnatory.

Unlike Jonah and many of us, God is not itching to get His hand on a hammer and batter all those evil people who do not follow His commands. Even around Jonah's time, we read that God took "no pleasure in the death of the wicked, but rather that they turn from their ways and live" (Ezek. 33:11). I believe God took greater delight in the 120,000 inhabitants of Nineveh who repented than in the killing by Gideon's army of the 120,000 Amalekite and Midianite soldiers (see Judg. 8:10). God wants us to be gracious and merciful as well toward those living around us, especially our fellow believers. In addition to burying the hatchet and uniting with other Christians to bring the message of salvation to our cities, we should be praying for and seeking ways to encourage its leaders. That is a much better way of ensuring "that we may live peaceful and quiet lives" (1 Tim. 2:2) than continually criticizing and complaining.

Aiming at the Leaders

Jonah's words of warning spread like a wildfire through the city of Nineveh. They reached the ears of people at every level of society, from the king to the lowest cowherd. The king was deeply moved and responded to Jonah's message. Repenting himself, he called on the city's inhabitants to do the same and appeal to God for mercy (see Jon. 3:6-9). Note that once the king repented, spiritual change swept through the rest of the city.

A similar phenomenon occurred when Paul preached in Corinth. The conversion of the influential ruler of the synagogue, Crispus, was a stimulus to many Corinthians to believe in Jesus (see Acts 18:8). Our prayers and concerns for the well-being of our cities' citizens should also include the political, financial, and business leaders. Not only is this our responsibility as law-abiding Christian inhabitants (see 1 Tim. 2:2; Titus 3:1), but these people owe their positions to God. Our prayers and support will enable them to make good and just decisions (see Rom. 13:1-5) and further the growth of God's Kingdom.

In his remarkable book, *Transformation,*[3] Ed Silvoso provides many accounts of how Christians have prayed for and contacted their political and business leaders, with dramatic spiritual, economic, and political results. There is Francis Oda, CEO of an architecture firm, who was asked for his opinion on a project by the president of Tahiti. The president was so impressed he gave Oda the job which stimulated the economic growth of the country—and the president eventually became a believer himself! Or Joan Simmons, the Bermudan businesswoman who successfully sought and gained an interview with her premier, recommended a national day of prayer, and was granted her request.

A friend of ours is a doctor and pastor in the south of the Netherlands. As in many places in Holland, his town had its *koffie shop,* where cannabis or marijuana was sold legally. On a normal day, 3,000 visitors came to buy drugs from as far away as France, generating sales of €40 million ($52.2 million) every year! Recognizing that this was a problem, representatives of several churches, including Reformed, Pentecostal, and Salvation Army, came together to pray for a change. Our friend lobbied the mayor and local council. Within a few months, the whole drugs business shut down, and the proprietors left. Many of the previous drug addicts are now active church members, and the mayor has considerable respect for the authority of the church leaders!

In Zagreb too, groups of Protestants and Roman Catholics have been praying for the political leaders of the nation. During this time, the then Minister of Science and Education became a believer, and the Prime Minister resigned and was arrested on corruption charges. New interdenominational prayer groups are now appearing, and young people are getting involved. God has given us an open door. We just have to enter it with expectant prayer.

Out Onto the Streets

To Jonah's amazement, the contrition and repentance was so extensive across the city of Nineveh that God relented from His intended judgment. Although no historical document records this remarkable moral and spiritual reversal, it is corroborated by Jesus (see Matt. 12:41; Luke 11:32). In fact, Jesus commends the people of Nineveh for heeding Jonah's warning, denouncing the cities of Galilee for their unbelief in response to His message (see Matt. 11:20-24). Jesus wept over Jerusalem (see Luke 19:41) and is still moved by compassion over the millions of people in our cities—from the road sweeper to the mayor—who desperately need the living hope He offers. Like the Street Pastors I mentioned earlier, we have to get out onto the streets and give the citizens the chance to respond.

As in many East European cities, the old socialist apartment blocks in Zagreb are not in the best of repair. No one sees them as their responsibility, and mutual agreement between residents is difficult to obtain. So nothing gets done. One Saturday, about forty believers and friends from several churches in the area got together and cleaned up the courtyard of one of the communal apartment buildings. This altruistic community cleanup made such an impression that the event was covered by the newspapers and national television! What is more, many new friends and contacts were made. United Christian love in action gets noticed.

We have to be flexible and adapt our approach to the local culture. In Zagreb, people are found in the cafés, in San Francisco down by Fisherman's Wharf, in New Delhi in the markets, in London in the pubs. And every city has its offices, factories, schools, colleges, and shops. *Are we reaching out to our fellow believers to build the fishing net of connections that will bring in the biggest catch the world has ever seen?* Near my hometown, one of the local Anglican fellowships moved out of their traditional, picturesque, square-towered church building. They now hold meetings in five local pubs to which they invite anybody who enters for a drink. Another church has a monthly men's breakfast in a guesthouse so the tourists also hear the Gospel while eating their scrambled eggs on toast! And the responses are all encouraging! People are hungry for the truth.

Jonah did not call the Ninevites to go on a pilgrimage to Jerusalem to gain forgiveness, any more than Jesus told the Samaritan woman to go and worship on Mount Zion (see John 4:19-24). In fact, He told the man in Decapolis, whom He delivered from multiple demons, to stay where he was and tell his family and friends about what Jesus had done for him (see Mark 5:18-20). Philip, also, after instructing and baptizing the eunuch in the desert, did not try to keep him from returning to Ethiopia (see Acts 8:26-39). (Indeed, it was the eunuch who watched Philip get caught up by the Spirit as they came up out of the water and be transported to another place!)

We have been trapped into the idea that we have to invite somebody to a formal service in our church building before they respond to the Gospel. Young Christians are encouraged to attend church activities three to four times a week or go to Bible School and become a full-time church worker. It may surprise you that this is not how the early disciples behaved or what Paul taught! Paul says clearly that young converts should not change their circumstances to fit in with their new Christian status, but rather allow the Holy Spirit to work through them to change the hearts and lives of their friends, colleagues, and relatives (see 1 Cor. 7:17-24). We have to go where the people are with all the help we can get from our fellow Christians.

Taking New Approaches

Despite being one of the most effective missionaries in history, Jonah could only think how unfair God was to be merciful to his enemies (see Jon. 4:2). He paid more attention to the way *he* expected

God to work than to what *God* intended. He was more concerned that the methods he used should prove correct than he was about the results, which were wildly greater than his methods could ever have predicted. Is that not just like many of our church activities? We are more concerned about making our approach denomination-ally appropriate than we are about seeing a wildfire of uncontrolled revival in our towns and cities. But God intends to work through His mercy and love, bringing blessing in ways we could not possibly have imagined. *God does not want us to restrict Him by the institutional and doctrinal principles we have imposed on Him.*

Jesus spent the whole of His ministry breaking down barriers, assumptions, and preconceived ideas. He shocked the academics by taking uneducated fishermen as His trainees. He offended the clerics' legalism by eating corn on the Sabbath. He crossed racial boundaries by helping a Samaritan woman. He instituted health-care reforms by touching and healing lepers and raising the dead. He upset social strata by associating with prostitutes and criminals, and He caused an economic upheaval by turning over the tables of the moneychangers in the temple. Is it not time to get out of the boat and expect the unimaginable with Jesus?

Do We Have the Heart for the Task?

God gave His prophet a lesson. Sitting on the hillside, Jonah expected a grandstand view of God's supernatural action. Willing God to destroy the city, he almost got heatstroke from the sun (see Jon. 4:5-6). So using the most effective fertilizer ever, God caused a vine to grow extremely rapidly to give him shade. But during the night, the plant was eaten by a worm and scorched by the hot wind, and Jonah defaulted to complaining mode. Totally uninterested in the fate of the Ninevites, Jonah's own comfort and the confirmation of his religious rectitude became paramount. "How is it," God reprimands, "that you are more concerned about losing a sunshade than about 120,000 people in this city?" (see Jon. 4:9-11). Here, the story ends, and we are not provided with the next installment.

In the absence of any historical record, all we know is that 100 years later—as told in the Book of Nahum—Nineveh was totally destroyed by the Babylonians because of its wickedness. What would have happened if Jonah had shared God's compassion for the city's inhabitants? What if he had trained and discipled some of the converts to be teachers? What if he had taken time to instruct the king in God's laws of justice and righteousness? What if he had gone back to Israel to get help from other prophets and priests? What if he had built a team to show God's practical love and concern to the city? How different its fate might have been!

Jonah performed the task he was given, but only to the letter of the word he had received from God. His heart was not in it; he had no passion for his ministry, no compassion for the city, and no interest in working with others to bring lasting change. Our Bible knowledge and attendance of church services will not bring spiritual breakthrough in our towns and cities. Nor will our attachment to ceremonies or our zeal for denominational purity. But our love for the Lord and His Family, our compassion for the needs of the people around us, and our responsiveness to God's heart and the leading of His Holy Spirit will.

Total Transformation

There is no doubt that God is drawing His Church together, challenging us all to change. A Global Day of Prayer at Pentecost each year brings millions together in intercession for the cities and nations of the world.[4] This annual event owes its existence to the initiative of the South African businessman, Graham Power. In March 2001, with his home city, Cape Town, undergoing severe social disturbances, he brought 45,000 believers together in a rugby football stadium to pray. As Ed Silvoso recounts, the violence stopped.[5] In the next couple of years, large prayer gatherings spread across South Africa, and by May 2004, to 56 countries around the world.

We need to get involved as well. There are cities out there waiting to learn about the love of Jesus. Jonah spent three days in a fish before bringing revival to the city of Nineveh. Jesus was three days in the grave before rising again and said of Himself, "One greater than Jonah is here" (Matt. 12:41). This same Jesus is living by His Spirit in each of us who believes, in His Body, the Church, so the effect of our message should be totally transformational. We have a message, a goal worth proclaiming: "When…the people of God are mobilised and work together to complete the task, then beyond our comprehension, beyond anything we can imagine, the glory of the Lord will come."[6]

It is not simply a question of setting up a new organization; there are plenty of groups that have done this on a grand scale. What I believe God is doing now is something greater, deeper, and more effective. He is calling grassroots, believing Christians, not just church leaders, to actively work together *by His Spirit*—not to agree on everything, but to combine our diversity to practically transform the hearts and lives of the people in the cities in which we live; to restore hope to the discouraged and give purpose and joy to those who are fearful of the future; to take back what the enemy has stolen and regain a moral compass for the nations. Jesus is the Way, the Truth, and the Life, and one day every knee is going to bow and confess Him as Lord. Till then, it is our task as His Body, the Church, to reveal His glory and love in our unity and practical love for one another and for the world He died to save.

ENDNOTES

1. http://encarta.msn.com/media_701500251/urban_population_growth.html; www.unfpa.org/swp/2007/english/chapter_1/index.html.

2. Henry Drummond, *The City Without a Church* (London, UK: Hodder and Stoughton, 1988), 12.

3. Ed Silvoso, *Transformation* (Ventura, CA: Regal Books, 2007).

4. http://www.globaldayofprayer.com/.

5. Silvoso, *Transformation*, 169.

6. Andrew Murray, cited in Stibbe and Williams, *Breakout*, 212.

About the Author

Mike Parnham is a British research pharmacologist and university teacher. His work, both at universities and as a manager and consultant for several companies, has taken him and his family to various countries across Europe, including England, the Netherlands, Germany, and Croatia. This mobility broadened the family's language, culture, and spiritual understanding.

Brought up in a conservative Evangelical environment, he has, during his career, been a lay preacher, teacher, deacon, and elder in Brethren, Baptist, Pentecostal, and Charismatic churches.

He and his wife, Elaine, a schoolteacher, lived for the past 13 years in Zagreb, Croatia, where their vision for Christian unity developed. They pursued this vision by helping organize interdenominational prayer meetings, home groups, and interchurch activities. Mike and Elaine live in Germany where he accepted a research position. They have four adult children (and one grandchild) who are also actively involved in different forms of church building in the United Kingdom and the Netherlands.

Additional copies of this book and other book
titles from EVANGELISTA MEDIA™
and DESTINY IMAGE™ EUROPE
are available at your local bookstore.

We are adding new titles every month!

To view our complete catalog online, visit us at:
www.evangelistamedia.com

Send a request for a catalog to:

**Via della Scafa, 29/14
65013 Città Sant'Angelo (Pe), ITALY
Tel. +39 085 4716623 • Fax +39 085 9090113
info@evangelistamedia.com**

"Changing the World, One Book at a Time"

Are you an author?

Do you have a "today" God-given message?

CONTACT US

We will be happy to review your manuscript
for the possibility of publication:

publisher@evangelistamedia.com
http://www.evangelistamedia.com/pages/AuthorsAppForm.htm